SO YOU'RE CAREER CONFUSED!

WTF IS NEXT?

PROVEN STEPS TO PINPOINT YOUR IDEAL CAREER DIRECTION

GREG WEISS

"So You're Career Confused! WTF Is Next?" by Greg Weiss

Published by Ingram Spark

www.wtfisnext.wtf

© *2019 Global Personal Consulting Pty Limited ACN 52 991 497 240*

For information about special discounts available for bulk purchases, sales promotions, fund-raising and educational needs, contact Global Personal Consulting Pty Limited or **sales@wtfisnext.wtf**

ISBN: 978-0-6484607-2-5

*To all the people I have coached over time,
I have grown by working with each and every one of you.*

*The process of leading you through your career
transition to a more meaningful and enriched life
has in its own way enriched my own.
For that, I am grateful.*

Illustrations by Sacha Rena

sacharena.com

WORDS OF THANKS

Thank you for picking up a copy of this book.

This year, I set about writing two books, the first to help new employees successfully get onboard with their new employer and pass their probation period, called **"So You Got The Job! WTF is Next?"**

The second is the book you have in your hands.

I was motivated to write **"So You're Career Confused! WTF Is Next?"** as about half the people who see me need some dedicated support and a practical system to help them determine their career direction.

My aim is to help you work out how to lead an enriched working life. After all, your work makes up the majority of your week. It might as well be one that you thoroughly enjoy, rather than loathe.

Your support means a lot to me.

If you find this book helpful, here are the best ways to help me spread the word:

1. Please leave a review of the book wherever you bought this book. Posting a review is easy and doesn't take much time. Detailed reviews help new readers discover how they too can benefit from this book.

2. Donate a copy to your local public library or institution of higher education or learning.

3. Give it as a gift to anyone you know who is career confused, whether they have just completed a qualification, are in between jobs or been forced out of work due to restructure performance.

If you have any questions, or you'd like to share how this book helped you, you can reach me via **gregw@wtfisnext.wtf**

To your enriched career!

Greg Weiss
July 2019

TABLE OF CONTENTS

INTRODUCTION

PART 1

Reboot

So you're career confused! As a career coach, about half the people I meet are too!

I want to congratulate you on picking up this book.

Deciding on a career direction can be a daunting task. You're facing the practicalities of choosing one that pays enough to maintain your lifestyle and feed you and if you have one, your family.

But once you've worked out your ideal career direction, there's also the emotional baggage and stress that seems to go hand-in-hand with the job search.

You're probably thinking about:

- If you are new to the job market, where to start and do you have what it takes?

- If you are working, then whether the unhappiness you're experiencing at your current job outweighs the stress of starting anew

- The injury to your pride and sense of identity if you've been let go

- What your friends and family will think of your career change

- Whether you have what it takes to move onward and upward

- When you will manage to land that coveted new position and whether it will actually be the right fit for you

- If you worked in the past, will you re-dedicate yourself to a similar role, just with a different employer? Or do you plan to start over by relaunching your career in a different direction?

But the thing at the forefront of your mind, whether you are new to the market or a seasoned employee is likely ... *where to start?*

Know that you don't need to decide this now. For that's what this book is designed to do ... help you figure out what your priorities are when it comes to a career and refine what you learn until you've reached a decision you're not only comfortable with but also excited about!

After all, it's one of those questions we've been asked from a young age - "what do you want to be when you grow up?" The truth is, most of us just don't know. What we want to "be" is far more elusive than the "calling" we all hoped would magically appear. What can be scary is that despite access to technology giving us more ways than ever to find a job vacancy, the length of the job search is getting longer. It's ironic but true. Statistics suggest it can take between four and six months to find a job.[1,2,3]

The average number of jobs millennials are expected to have across their career is estimated to be between 15 and 20.[4] But don't be disheartened. The good news is this decreases the pressure to find that one perfect career for the majority of your life. There is no one right answer! Instead, you have multiple opportunities for reinvention.

This brings us to the idea of long term employability vs. long term employment.

LONG TERM EMPLOYABILITY VS. LONG TERM EMPLOYMENT

This decade, we've seen articles published bearing headlines like "Is Workplace Loyalty Dead?"[5] or the even more alarmist "Long Term Employment is Dead."[6]

One thing is certain. The working environment has undergone significant changes throughout the generations, from the baby boomers through Gen X and to the millennial generation - so it's not surprising some are finding this quite an adjustment.

Career goals used to consist of finding a company where you could work hard for 20 years or more, and then be rewarded for your efforts. However, the "quid pro quo of modern employment is more likely to be:

As long as I work for you, I promise to have the relevant skills and engage fully in my work; in return you'll pay me fairly, but I don't expect you to care for me when I'm 110."[7]

In our fast-paced world, the length of tenure is cast aside for a focus on more flexible and engaged employees. After all, those who have been in one position for a long time are not necessarily more engaged and productive than those newer to the company.[8]

So why has the workforce changed so significantly?

Well, there are several factors. According to Thomas Friedman, author of *The World is Flat*, there are ten "flatteners" that have levelled the global playing field. Of these, we're going to touch on three factors specifically:

1. **Outsourcing:** the ability to outsource work has provided the most cost-effective and efficient means of fulfilling individual components of service and manufacturing activities. Whether an employer now hires a single freelancer or has their entire manufacturing process completed by a third-party, we've seen significant changes to how we work that were once never even imagined.

2. **Offshoring:** the ability to take advantage of lower-cost operations in other countries has made businesses more competitive, diverse and can operate on a broader scale.

3. **Technology:** the rise of digitisation, the internet, workflow software and supply chaining have come to mean that some tasks no longer require human involvement. Processes such as streamlined sales, distribution and shipping may not need as many people to conduct operations. And those that are involved are likely to be in different roles, like quality control or in a supervisory capacity, rather than a traditional hands-on role.[9]

Our technological prowess has created a fast-paced economy, where the pace of change is indeed one to be in awe of. To put this in perspective, consider Buckminster Fuller's "knowledge-doubling curve" of

1982. This showed that back in 1900, our knowledge was doubling every century. Fast-forward to 1982 and knowledge was doubling every 12-13 months. That's an astounding leap forward. IBM has since added post-1982 predictions, that knowledge is doubling every 12-13 hours.[10]

It's this immense surge in knowledge from 1982 on, that has seen all these factors we've just mentioned (outsourcing, offshoring and technology) become an everyday reality in our truly global marketplace.

This is *your* reality.

But while arguments abound that the modern workforce lacks loyalty and stability, it's certainly not all bad news. Because some believe that long-term, full-time employment with just a couple of employers can actually hold you back. Here's why:

1. You have a stagnant resume[11] with few "Dragon-Slaying Stories" that you can use to ace your job interviews.[12] These are the stories about problems you solved in previous positions, that demonstrate what an asset you are. Of course, (without suggesting you become too erratic in your career) the more positions you've held, the more varied your experiences and stories will be.

2. You effectively work inside a box.[13] There is little opportunity for growth unless your employer dictates it. This affects you day to day, but also in terms of long-term professional opportunities.

3. You identify yourself only by your job title when in reality, you are so much more than just your position in the workforce.[14]

4. You become a "limited" expert in only those tasks you must fulfil for your role and for that employer. You can grow out of touch with the industry and even the clients you're serving because you effectively become blinkered.

5. The job search is much more difficult next time around. And you should be prepared so there will be a next time.

Long-term, stable positions still exist. But if you're open to options and willing to explore what the modern workforce has to offer, you'll have a better chance of finding yourself on the path to a career that fulfils and excites you.

That's why I advocate for the idea of long-term employability. This means your focus is on evolving your skills throughout your working life so that you remain employable, instead of the traditional focus on having a long-term employment contract.

ALLOW YOURSELF TO BE CURIOUS

As you move through life, it's natural to become hyper-focused on the responsibilities you assume, and the routines you build, forgetting to be curious about new experiences. And some people may see the realities of the labour market today as restrictive. But they don't have to be.

You now have more resources at your disposal and the freedom to be more curious about the possibilities than ever before. Philosopher and civil rights leader Howard W. Thurman said, "ask what makes you come alive and go do it."[15] Embrace the opportunity at hand, and use this book to figure out that balance between what you'd like to do and what you can do.

THIS BOOK IS FOR YOU

I've written this book so that you too can benefit from exploring who you are now, in order to determine

your ideal career pathway. You deserve to have the tools to find a job that not only meets your needs but also satisfies your values and interests.

In this book, you'll discover:

- How to take stock of where you are right now
- How to deal with the mental and emotional anguish of losing a job, moving on from a prior workplace or missing out on the job you really wanted
- How to develop strategies for a positive approach to the job search
- Clues to your future direction, based on your past experiences
- What's really important to you - in life and career
- Where you naturally fit and the people with whom you are most comfortable
- How to find the enriched space at the intersection of where your strengths lie, what you love, what's important to you and what is a financially-viable career
- How to sidestep common career traps and learn the secrets to an enriched career
- How to convey who you are and go after what you really want

Unlike many aptitude tests or career-finding resources, this book is designed to:

- Be easy to digest. Information is drip-fed in a process-driven format to guide you every step of the way
- Help you find the right balance between wants and needs, practicality and passion
- Give you time for self-reflection, without requiring you to write lengthy journals or essays

What would moving on from your previous or current position to find your ideal career mean to you? Would it feel as though:

- "My human element hasn't been forgotten, and I'm no longer just a number."
- "I receive faster feedback and can be more confident in my role."
- "I have an improved work/life balance."
- "I have better opportunities for growth."
- "I have more creative leeway."
- "I finally have a job I 'want' to do, not just have to do."

WHO AM I TO HELP YOU

For most of my working career, I have helped managers and executives accelerate and relaunch their careers.

I am known for being an entrepreneur, especially

within the HR profession. I have started (and sold) several HR-related businesses from executive search and recruitment; to employee engagement and retention; to HR Director level development and networking.

I am the author of **So You Got The Job! WTF Is Next?** a book proven to help new employees improve their chances of surviving the risky first three months by 69 per cent.

I also founded CareerSupport365.com which provides career transitioning support services that allow departing employees to be equipped with the knowledge, skills and attitudes empowering them to work out where they will be happy in their next career move.

SUCCESS STORIES

Rhianna completed a Science-based degree. Within a short while, it occurred to her that she had studied the wrong course and was working within the wrong profession.

Feeling depleted and admitting to having studied the sciences due to parental pressure, she yearned for something much bigger from work. She was career confused.

After a few coaching sessions with me, it was clear that Rhianna wanted to make a difference to people, but not based on the path her studies traditionally paved. Instead she decided her life would be much more enriched if she dedicated her focus to the social impact sector.

Applying the exercises in this book, especially on creating a compelling story, Rhianna applied for a top course abroad and despite stiff competition, was accepted. Returning home, she was employed in the social impact sector and is now living her enriched life.

_____

When I met John for our first career coaching session, he looked defeated and on the verge of depression.

John had been dismissed by his employer due to poor performance. Most recently holding a Claims role for an insurance company, when he presented for his first session with me, everything about him was grey and depleted. He hated his job and everything about it.

So it was no surprise that he was performance managed out by his employer.

In our first meeting, I introduced John to the frameworks included in this book. By the end of our meeting, John's entire physiology changed to a someone with hope and excitement. His greyness had already started to lift.

3 weeks after his redundancy, and having deeply worked on the SLIMPACT™ model in this book, John accepted the offer of a job working in an industry for which he had a real love, where he harnessed many of his strengths. Last I spoke with him, John is happily employed and in hindsight, considers his dismissal a gift.

WHY THIS BOOK, WHY NOW?

You might be wondering, why is this the best time to set out on a path of career discovery?

Firstly, there's the myth that the 'grass is always greener'. While this isn't a new concept, unfortunately, social media has enhanced it so that we are tempted to think we are missing out if we don't have one of those glamorous laptop, travel and sunset lifestyles. It's important to remember that how others present their careers isn't necessarily realistic, nor do they tell you the downsides. There are pros and cons to every career after all! That's why it's important not to just grasp at straws because something looks appealing but find out what's right for you.

Secondly, we are quite literally spoiled for choice. While we're lucky to have more opportunities than ever, it can make it tricky to figure out which way to turn. That's why it's important to self-analyse, by putting the effort in to figure out where your skills, interests and values really lie.

Finally, there's the tremendous fear of the future that's ingrained into our culture. "The time is now!" "Do it before it's too late!" everyone cries, filling us with this sense of pressure that if we don't do everything right (and right now), we will only regret it later.[16] The race to the top mentality isn't always as rewarding as we're led to believe. Have you ever achieved something just to feel a little numb once you do and then wonder where are the feelings of elation you expected? Maybe it's okay to do a little less as long as you do it for enjoyment and lead a contented life.

Ultimately, the purpose of this book is to help you identify a career that will enrich your life with vitality.

HOW TO USE THIS BOOK

This book will guide you through a process that

will not only help you determine your ideal career direction, but also help you deal with the sometimes unexpected feelings of loss that can come from moving on.

This isn't a book you devour once, put down and expect results. Instead, it's a specially-designed process for you to work through. As you read each chapter, you will find activities to help you implement what you have just read. These are supported by examples and case studies all designed to help you make the most of each new topic that we cover.

If you are serious about finding a new job that isn't just a american spelling, it's essential to complete each chapter before moving onto the next.

Working on your SLIMPACT™ is the most critical lesson contained within this book for finding a career that contributes to an overall enriched and fulfilled life, rather than a depleted one. But it is essential that you move sequentially through the book completing its activities and exercises.

I wish you well as you read this book and enjoy a better chance of finding career fulfilment.

Please let me know how your path to career discovery goes. Email me at: **gregw@wtfisnext.wtf**

CHAPTER 1

COPE WITH CHANGE

PART 1

Reboot

Let's talk about change.

We're living in a time where so much about our work is shifting, including our ideals. According to psychiatrist Gabriela Cora, the preference we once had for stability has transformed so that today, what you look for in a career might be more akin to a "calling". In particular, this change in ideals shows up as a drive to create something new or do something interesting.[1]

Dr Jean Twenge led a generational study of high school seniors and found that millennials, Gen X and Baby Boomers all place a high value on having an "interesting" job. But Boomers can have trouble breaking with the traditional mould thanks to financial concerns, so they may instead encourage the younger generations to seek interesting work, rather than pursue it themselves.[2]

So, there's a shift in ideals, but there's also a transformation in the rigours of traditional work that makes it seem less attractive. That's because jobs and employers are more demanding of us than ever before, and the rewards are few and far between. That means less autonomy and more tediousness - it really has become the daily grind. Even more off-putting is that there doesn't seem to be any compensation for this less fulfilling work.[3]

If you are just starting out in your career, these changes to the workforce may not be your primary concern. Rather, it will be the change from studying (whether at a secondary or tertiary level) to working.

For you, the shift will be in terms of managing an increased level of responsibility, an adjustment in your identity - from student to employee - and possibly, a struggle with what is called 'imposter syndrome' that may go along with that.

We will be exploring all aspects of change, no matter your work history, in the coming chapters. To prevent confusion, I will refer to this as "occupational" change, which applies to those not just dealing with a change of job, but also the shift from student to employee.

WHY IS CHANGE SO DIFFICULT?

There are two sides to the fear of change. Those are fear of uncertainty and fear of loss. When your occupational situation changes, voluntarily or not, both uncertainty and loss are sure to follow.

There is no way to guarantee the outcome when you lose or leave your job or finish studying. That's scary because you inevitably doubt if things will work out.

And even if you really desire the change, you are still opening up to losing a multitude of things that were tied up in your previous role.

Change, and therefore loss, is so difficult to bear because you're wired to protect what you've got. That's an ingrained survival instinct.

The thing about change is it often leads (in the long-term) to a sense of "that was the best thing that ever happened to me". Unfortunately, it rarely feels like that while you are experiencing it, and so we're often blind to the opportunities that open up as the loss occurs.

THE EMOTIONAL EXPERIENCE OF LOSS

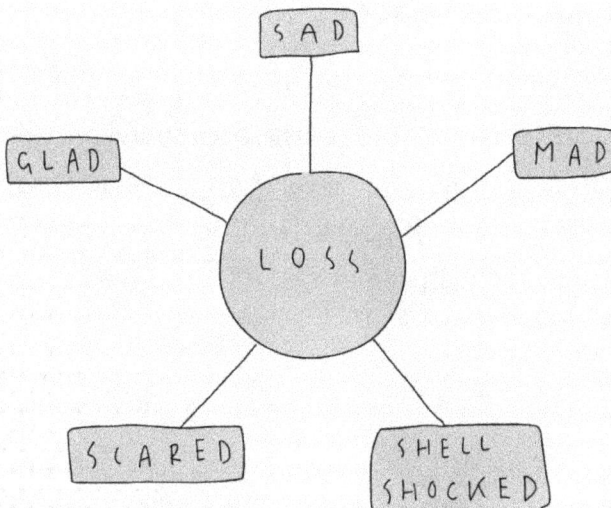

Whether your occupational change has come about willingly or not, there's a certain amount of emotional baggage that can affect where you go from here. In fact, you probably feel one or several of these:

Sad

It's upsetting when you're forcibly excluded from a workplace where you felt like you were trying your best. But it's also upsetting if you've decided to leave a job of your own accord, whether it was a happy one or not. It's sad to leave behind co-workers you've worked alongside with, day in, day out. It can even be hard to move on from customers that you've gone out of your way to help, and as a result, formed with them great relationships.

Similarly, when you're entering the workforce after study, you're forced to separate from your former classmates, the study environment and routines. If you particularly enjoyed studying, you may find this even more difficult.

Mad

If you've been let go, you are going to be angry. Angry at your employer for not giving you a fair go.

Angry at your co-workers for not supporting you enough. Angry at yourself because if you've been fired, you are probably beating yourself up and feeling like you failed. Maybe you're angry at the world because this happened to you and it was outside your control.

If you're taking on your first professional job after high school or university, you may experience anger at yourself for not living up to your expectations for your final results and where that would position you for work. You may even feel as though those teaching you didn't prepare you enough for the world of work.

Glad

When an occupational or student role isn't the right fit for you, you'll be happy to move on, whether it's of your own choosing or not. Even if the entire change isn't a happy one, you might find elements of relief in not having to:

- Work or study alongside a particular person
- Perform an undesirable task
- Get away from a workspace or study environment that you never felt at home in
- Remain in roles that others have cast you in,

giving you a chance to develop a new identity

Although you're fearful of what the future holds, some part of you is happy to embrace the freedom you now have in seeking a better opportunity.

Scared

The unknown scares us all. When you're cast back into the job search pool *or* you're diving in for the first time, you'll be plagued by questions like:

- "How long will it take me to find a job?"
- "What if I find it's harder than I expected?"
- "What if I don't like any of the opportunities and have to settle?"

You might be scared of letting your family down, fearful how people will react to your changing situation or even scared that you won't achieve your goals.

Shell shocked

While triggers for Post Traumatic Stress Disorder (PTSD) are classed as extreme events, a less intense but unpleasant experience can also trigger PTSD-like symptoms. These may include distress, a racing heart, irritability and insomnia to name a few.[4]

Therefore, it's not unreasonable to feel as though you are shell shocked when experiencing an emotionally disturbing event like job loss.

Similarly, as a graduating student you might experience symptoms like these if your student career didn't end on the high note you were expecting. Perhaps some of your final grades were disappointing and it's left you far short of the position you expected to be in. Perhaps everyone around you already has a job lined up and you're left feeling alone or even facing the reality of moving back home. Any unpleasant experiences like these can leave you feeling rather shell shocked.

ACTION STEPS

Take a moment to identify which of these five emotions (sad, mad, glad, scared or shell shocked) you are experiencing and note how they are showing up in your daily life.

_____

_____

_____

_____

_____

_____

THE OTHER LOSSES THAT COME FROM A CHANGE OF OCCUPATION

Losing or leaving a job, or finishing study, doesn't mean you're dealing with only the feelings tied up in the loss of the role itself. It's more complicated than that. According to HelpGuide.org, an occupational loss comes with a host of other losses, including loss of:[5]

- Professional identity or how you identified as a student
- Self-esteem and self-confidence
- A daily routine
- Purposeful activity
- A work-based social network
- Your sense of security

Let's take a closer look at how these may be affecting you.

Professional identity

Your sense of identity and professional pride is so bound up in what you do. It's tied to:

- Your position (in the workplace or as a student)
- The company or school you are part of
- Your organisational or group affiliations

When you enter a transition period, moving forward is the only way to disentangle yourself. You should start reaching out to people beyond the identity you've been clinging to. Then, you will begin to realise that you can be happy as your identity evolves and you learn to define yourself in different ways - either in the context of a different role, or from a student to a member of the workforce.

You probably want to start redefining yourself and getting clear on your new professional identity as soon as your transition begins, but the truth is, you haven't lived it yet, so you mustn't be disappointed upon realising it is a process and takes time.

Self-esteem

Redundancy or an unexpected exit unwittingly results in people internalising and personalising job loss, even though it's an economic reality. Job loss impacts your expectations of yourself (and might cause you to worry about how other people's expectations of you will be affected), and so your self-worth suffers.

As a graduate, the most significant risk to your self-esteem comes from imposter syndrome. Because you are most likely entering a company as the most

inexperienced person there, you may be worried that you aren't good enough or deserving enough to be there.

Daily routine

It's essential for your mental health to have something to get out of bed for. Some people may feel an initial elation at not having to get up for work or study, but this won't last long. The very presence of a routine is also important. Its structure and familiarity help you make sense of your everyday life.

When you don't have a routine, you lack direction. This can bring on anxiety, and it also means you need to rely on willpower to get anything done, rather than force of habit. When you lose momentum, it's that much harder to get going again - just like that feeling of trying to get back into the swing of work or study after an incredible holiday break.

The habits and patterns that stood you well in your previous role may no longer be a good fit (like stopping at your favourite cafe every day on the way to work, or behaving in a certain way around your classmates). You'll miss the psychological comfort and relief they once brought you, but it is a necessity that you break with them if they do not suit your new career phase.

Purposeful activity

Purposeful activity helps you create meaning from your life. It makes you feel like you're contributing to society and plays a large role in building your self-worth. When you lose purposeful activity from your life, you feel as though you are floundering. Without the enforced activity that comes with a job or study, you might need to remind yourself of the other ways you contribute, whether that's to a sporting team or a community cause.

Work or school-based social network

As well as fear of loss, you may also feel a sense of guilt if your occupational transition is voluntary. Leaving behind a company, your workmates, classmates and valued customers can feel much like leaving them in the lurch. So you might be worried about how your going may impact them. Even worse is when this feeling is voiced by your employer, embittered that you are moving on. It's an emotional challenge, but it's important to do what is right for you.[6]

Sense of security

It's not just your regular wage that is impacted for the here and now. Like wondering how to pay the

bills, put food on the table and continue the lifestyle your family is used to.

You can also feel you've lost your sense of security for everything you'd planned for your future - paying off your mortgage, giving your kids a head start at university and taking that round-the-country road trip you've been dreaming of.

According to London Business School professor, Herminia Ibarra, even when you leave voluntarily and for something you're excited about pursuing, it's still a loss.[7]

Making sense of the situation

A report published by Dell Technologies has estimated that a staggering 85% of jobs that will exist in 2030 haven't even been invented.[8]

Change is inevitable. It's how you cope with it that matters. So, let's take a look at how you might react.

According to Elisabeth Kubler-Ross, there are four stages of reacting to change:[9]

CHANGE

START

shock and disorientation

anger and other emotion responces

coming to terms with new situation

acceptance and moving forward

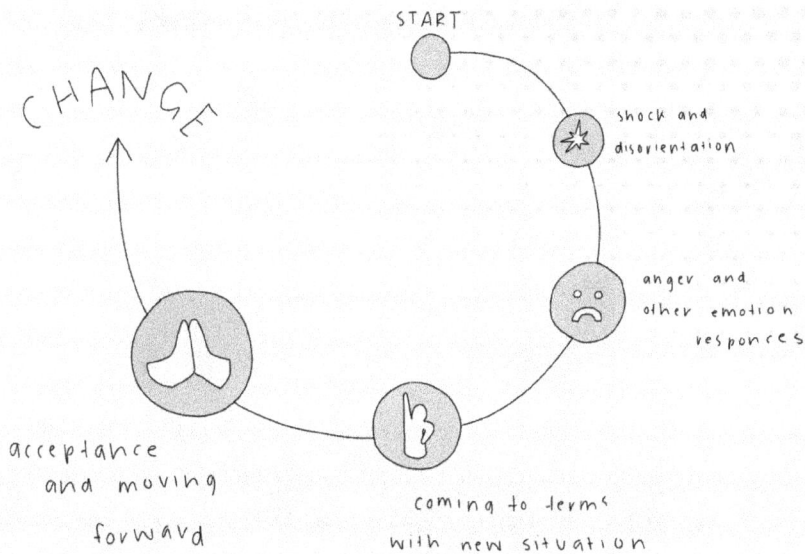

① Shock and disorientation

When the news is fresh, you won't be able to see a logical path forward. You'll be reeling as your mind races to uncover all the ways this is going to affect your life. It will take time to make sense of the situation.

② Anger and other emotional responses

Much like the five stages of grief, you'll progress through a range of emotions that you will need to feel before you can entirely move on with your life. The key to this stage is managing your strong feelings, without suppressing them. More on this in Chapter 2.

③ Coming to terms with the new situation

In this stage, you'll start to develop strategies for applying yourself in a new direction. A more optimistic outlook will help you explore how this change could lead to new opportunities. More on this in Chapter 3.

④ Acceptance and moving forward

It's time to realise that you learned much from your previous experience, and now good things await. You have a plan of attack for the future, and you are ready to follow it. More on this in Chapter 3.

PRACTICAL STEPS TO KEEP THINGS IN PERSPECTIVE

Even when you start to understand the inner mechanisms at work when you're dealing with occupational loss, it can be difficult to keep these front of your mind when you're struggling. That's why I suggest you try implementing these simple steps when you're struggling to keep your transition in perspective:

(1) Embrace humour to deal with stress or tension.

Make time to laugh every day. That could mean watching a funny video, playing a game with your kids or telling your spouse a funny story.

(2) Use your real-life social network.

They want to make you feel better, and you should let them try. They also have the benefit of an outside perspective too, so they may be able to see opportunities that you've overlooked.

(3) Focus on what you have achieved.

Consider everything you accomplished and all your contributions during your time with the company, school or training facility. Reminding yourself of the things that have enriched your life so far, helps to counter negative thoughts that may deplete your energy. Even when you leave, your achievements should not be discounted. Your layoff or decision to move on doesn't negate everything that came before.

4 COPE WITH CHANGE

ACTION STEPS

1. Embrace humor. What did you do to embrace humor today?

_____
_____
_____
_____
_____

2. Use your real-life social network. What did you do to reach out to friends and family this week?

_____
_____
_____
_____
_____

3. Focus on what you've achieved. What did you accomplish in your last role?

_____
_____
_____
_____
_____

If you can overcome your initial reaction to cling to what you have, you can embrace the positive aspects of change. It's not easy, but it's certainly possible. And ultimately, this opens you up to new possibilities for success.

KEY LESSONS

As you begin to grasp how this change may be affecting you, I encourage you to revisit these lessons from the chapter you just read.

It's natural for any kind of change to take time to adjust to. After all, change often means experiencing uncertainty and loss. Change, when it relates to an occupational situation, can also give rise to one or more of these emotions:

- Sad
- Mad
- Glad
- Scared
- Shellshocked

For it's not just the job you've lost (or left), or the study you're moving on from, you're experiencing loss in many related areas too:

- Professional identity
- Self-esteem and self-confidence
- A daily routine
- Purposeful activity
- A work or school-based social network
- Your sense of security

When you start to realise just how much of your life may change because of your occupational transition, you'll go through four stages:

1. Shock and disorientation
2. Anger and other emotional responses
3. Coming to terms with the new situation
4. Acceptance and moving forward

Throughout your transition, the most important thing you can try to do is maintain perspective. Using ways to relieve tension and focus on what you have achieved will help you begin to move forward, through this challenging period and into the opportunities beyond.

Chapter 2 brings a deep-dive into the grief-like process you may be working through and a guide to healthily dealing with these emotions.

CHAPTER 2

STRATEGIES FOR ACCEPTANCE

PART 1

Reboot

2
STRATEGIES FOR ACCEPTANCE

Now that you've made some sense of your situation and looked at how you've been coping so far, it's time to start grappling with the emotions that are showing up for you. Moving on from a workplace or place of study that you've invested months or years of your life to, doesn't just bring up some mild discomfort. Often, the feelings you experiences are intense - like those usually associated with the grieving process.

It may seem strange to compare the loss of an occupation with that of a person. And in no way do I mean to be insensitive and imply that they are indeed the same thing. But, what is true, is that coping with each of these life events requires progressing through stages of emotion that affect many aspects of your life, and it takes time. The journey is different for each person and their individual circumstances.

The Kubler-Ross model (the five stages of grief), was developed to help doctors understand the emotions of their dying patients and those experiencing bereavement.[1] Whether you're moving on from a previous job or entering the workforce as a recent graduate, let's look at how this applies to your situation and some strategies to help you reach a state of acceptance more easily.

OCCUPATIONAL LOSS AND THE STAGES OF GRIEF

If you're familiar with the Kubler-Ross model, you may have also heard of the five stages of grief referred to as DABDA, which stands for Denial, Anger, Bargaining, Depression and Acceptance. Keep in mind the stages are not necessarily linear, and you may not go through all of them.

D enial

A nger

B argaining

D epression

A cceptance

Denial

Typically, denial is the immediate response when experiencing loss. You may deny the facts in front of you, often refusing to accept your new reality.

Dr Russ Harris calls this the reality slap - when you've been hit out of nowhere by one of life's painful blows.[2]

A reality slap brings uncertainty - and uncertainty brings fear. When you lose something important to you, you may very well be afraid of what will happen next. The unknown is a scary place. It's no wonder your first instinct might be to bury your head in the sand and pretend it's not happening.

When staring into the abyss of the unknown, you can take some comfort in knowing that there is a way to alleviate the fear. And that is to get information.

Psychologists often ask patients to explore worst-case scenarios in detail. As hard as it may be to believe, thinking through these scenarios often provide people with freedom from their fears.

If you need to take a beat when the reality slap strikes - that's okay. Do it if you're at risk of being overwhelmed. It's important to be kind to yourself after all. But ensure you start taking action to move forward or seek professional help if you can't move out from under that cloud and are at risk of becoming depressed.

Anger

When denial ends, anger takes over. This is a potent physiological reaction to feeling threatened. Chemical responses in your brain start occurring the instant you feel angry.

These changes make rational thought difficult. It's understandable to want to find someone to blame so you have somewhere to direct your anger - whether inward or outward.

The trouble is, anger drives away positive results as well as the people you need most. Internalising it and blaming yourself can only affect your health in a negative way. Adrenaline and cortisol course through your body every time you get angry. Over time, repeated prolonged exposure to these chemicals can raise your blood pressure, weaken your immune system and even cause heart disease and ulcers.

But being openly angry or criticising your former employer and colleagues can have other repercussions like damaging your career, alienating your professional network and burning bridges for future opportunities.

Instead, you need to use your anger to propel you

toward healthy change. You can't banish anger from your life completely, and you shouldn't try to. But you need to learn how to manage it, instead of letting it control you. Use it to motivate yourself to change your circumstances.

ACTION STEPS

Anger journal

An anger journal can help you understand and manage your anger. Keeping an anger journal takes no more than a few minutes a day.

For the next 14 days, take a small notebook, and whenever you find yourself angry, answer the following questions. At the end of the day, note how many anger incidents you experienced. Over these two weeks, see if you can uncover your anger triggers – the people or places that make you most angry. Once you find your triggers, you can take steps to avoid them and manage your anger more effectively.

1. Where are you?

_____

_____

_____

_____

_____

2. What made you angry?

_____
_____
_____
_____
_____
_____

3. How angry are you, on a scale of 1 (a little irritated) to 10 (so furious you can't speak)?

_____
_____
_____
_____
_____
_____

4. What do you think are your anger triggers so that you can take steps to avoid them and manage your anger more effectively?

_____
_____
_____
_____
_____
_____

Bargaining

In this stage, you may try to delay the inevitable and negotiate a different outcome.

If you are faced with job loss, you may attempt to negotiate with your employer to give you another chance or allow you to remain at work part-time. You may even try to strike a bargain with God, giving yourself false hope that your joblessness will somehow be avoided.

It's also common to find yourself plagued with "what if" statements like:

- "What if I hadn't missed that deadline last year"?
- "What if I'd made more effort to socialise with the boss?"
- "What if I'd done more overtime throughout our busy period?"

"Surely I wouldn't have been let go then?"

If you are a graduating student, you won't be dealing with job loss, but rather, the apprehension in moving on to a career.

In this case, you may be tempted to extend your studies and undertake a further degree to remain secure in your identity as a student and delay entering the workforce.

You might be thinking:

"What if I had been more dedicated to my studies and achieved better grades?"

"What if I had spent more time planning my future?"

"Surely I'd feel more prepared than I do now?"

In the bargaining stage, you remain locked into the past of "what might have been." But you can't stay here.

Depression (and post-graduate depression)

When sadness, regret and uncertainty begin to set in, this indicates that acceptance of your new reality is starting. Commonly, you will feel empty or numb, and it feels natural to withdraw. Things can seem overwhelming, to the point of hopelessness. At this stage, you are living life passively, and it can be difficult to motivate yourself to find your career direction.

Depression is the stage most likely to apply to recent graduates. In fact, this has been coined "post-graduate depression." This may show up for you because of any number of reasons:

- The extensive planning and anticipation leading to final exams are over

- You feel "let down" when the great transformation you expected in yourself at graduation doesn't seem to have happened

- You feel empty because you haven't set any concrete goals beyond graduation[3]

- You're leaving behind an entire world and tight-knit community you shaped for yourself

- You may be concerned that the degree you worked so hard for, won't get you the job you expected

- You're confused because graduation is meant to be a happy time, and it's difficult to admit it isn't that way for you

- The struggles of the "real world" can be completely different from those you faced while studying[4]

According to the National Alliance on Mental Health, young adulthood is a particularly vulnerable time, as "75 per cent of mental-health conditions begin by age 24."[5]

75%

of mental health conditions begin by 24

It's important to accept these low feelings, but you certainly shouldn't be at their mercy.

Next time you catch yourself feeling depressed, decide on a set period of time to experience that feeling fully. It could be 5, 10, or even 30 minutes. Set a timer, and for that amount of time, truly let yourself wallow in your feelings. You can write, yell, talk, or do anything else that allows you to feel everything you need to feel. When the timer goes off, however, it's time to stop.

Of course, your feelings won't immediately go away, but you'll stop focusing on the negative and do something constructive or practical. In addition, every time you use this timer activity, be sure to take 5 minutes afterwards to check in with yourself.

Note what triggered your feelings of depression, how long you set the timer for, what you did, and how you felt afterwards. Over time, you'll start to see patterns – and hopefully, you'll be able to avoid the triggers, shorten the amount of time you need to be depressed, and feel better afterwards.

ACTION STEPS

Feeling low

1. Let your feelings out.

_____
_____
_____
_____
_____
_____

2. What triggered those feelings?

_____
_____
_____
_____
_____
_____

3. How could you avoid them or reduce the frequency of feeling them?

_____

_____

_____

_____

_____

_____

Acceptance

Reaching positive acceptance provides a sense of stability and often, calm objectivity. When you've reached the acceptance stage, you will be well and truly ready to begin a new role without dragging the emotional baggage of your loss with you.

Once you've reached this stage, it's essential to anchor yourself here, so that you don't risk sliding backward if you experience setbacks in your job search. I'll introduce you to strategies that will help you keep moving in this positive direction, particularly, by anticipating your success (see Chapter 3).

You may or may not relate to what you see in the five stages, but the important thing is to know there is a reason you're feeling whatever you're feeling. If you're having difficulty accepting your loss, you'll find yourself in a better place if you let your emotions run their course.

The key to transforming your outlook is not to try to force your feelings into behaving. You're not supposed to feel a specific way so repressing yourself won't help. Let yourself feel what you are feeling. It's completely legitimate. At the same time, you don't want to wallow in despair without hope for recovery.

HOW GRIEVING CAN AFFECT YOUR HEALTH

One significant reason why you should not wallow in the grief of your occupational change is the effect it can have on your health. You might assume these impacts are just on your mental health, but unfortunately, it's well-documented that it can extend to your physical health too.

You've probably heard about executives working in extremely stressful roles suffering from hypertension, heart disease or even diabetes. The same applies to those who find themselves suddenly unemployed, or between study and the next stage of their life.

In fact, a study from 1999-2003 by sociologist Kate Strully, found that of unemployed people who previously had no health concerns before their job loss, "80% were diagnosed with a new health problem ... 18 months later." Even those who were gainfully "re-employed within a year and a half also reported increased onset of new health problems."[6]

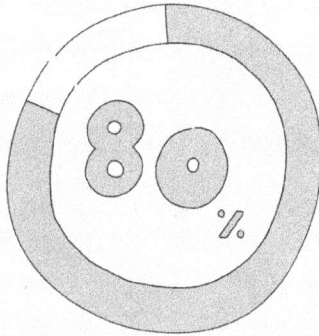

of unemployed people
were diagnosed with a
new health problem 18
months later

Looking after yourself in this time is critical. You'll find out more in the next chapter about how to stay healthy as you decide your new direction.

THE IMPORTANCE OF REFRAMING

Expert positive psychologists teach the importance of not fusing with your situation. Fusing to your situation means accepting it as the reality of who you are.[7] For instance, you have fused with your job loss or inability to find employment if you say "I am unemployed". Rather, you should step back and say "right now I am in a situation where I am without a job." There are fine, but very powerful distinctions in these statements.

That's where reframing, and the heart of it, language, comes in. Instead of talking about loss, turn the conversation to your "occupational change."

See the difference?

One way to reframe your situation is to think about where you'll be going next in your career. In a job interview, the way you describe the turns your career have taken make a big impression.

If an interviewer asks you, "Why were you laid off?" your response might be, "The company was forced to consolidate resources as part of a larger strategic plan. My goal now is ..." This points to what your plan is going forward, rather than dwelling on the discomfort of the past.

Imagine the questions you may be asked in interviews, and think about how you can recast the situation in a more positive light – while maintaining honesty, of course.

In the same way, recognising where you are at in the five stages of grief is very helpful. So rather than fusing with "I am angry" you're better off reframing this by:

a) acknowledging where you are in the cycle at any given point

b) saying to yourself "right now I am feeling angry about my current situation, and I am determined that this will pass."

ACTION STEPS

Reframing

Practice this skill regularly. Anytime you encounter a challenge, try to reframe it as an opportunity. How would you consider reframing your situation?

_____
_____
_____
_____
_____

KEY LESSONS

As you move through the stages of grief and reach acceptance, I encourage you to revisit these lessons from the chapter you just read.

Although the Kubler-Ross model was originally developed for understanding the feelings related to the loss of people, it is still useful to apply in your situation. That's because job loss and the post-graduation period can also bring up strong emotions like denial, anger, bargaining and depression before reaching acceptance.

You may not experience all of them, or have them show up in that order. But the most important lesson is, that you should never suppress how you feel, just take care not to wallow. For the feelings associated with grief can be detrimental to your mental health, physical health and even your future career prospects.

If you tend to have a pessimistic approach to life, one way to help you redirect your thoughts is by using the reframing technique.

For instance, instead of saying "I am unemployed," it's more helpful to say "right now I am in a situation where I am without a job."

When you use reframing language (whether out loud or to yourself), that indicates you know the situation will pass, you believe it, and you change the narrative to one you have control over.

Chapter 3 brings strategies to help you develop the right mindset as the grieving process ends and your exploration of your future enriched career begins.

CHAPTER 3

ANTICIPATE SUCCESS

PART 1

Reboot

By this point, you've learned how to get a handle on your changing situation and cope with the emotional disturbance. Now it's time to move into the right mindset as you start to discover your best path forward.

But, what is the right mindset?

It's one that:

- Anticipates success
- Is future-focused
- Identifies a rich and meaningful life as true happiness
- Practices resilience
- Is open to opportunity

STAY FUTURE-FOCUSED

The first time you stood up, you probably fell down. The first time you tried to walk, you most likely toppled over. But because you didn't recognise the possibility of failure, you got up and tried again.

If you don't believe in your chance for success, you'll give up at the first sign of hardship, says Siimon Reynolds, the author of *Why People Fail*.[1]

Much like the language you use, your thoughts have

a profound impact on what you do. You can quite easily set yourself up for failure by exaggerating the size and severity of the problem you're facing, and by refusing to believe that you can change your situation.

Fortunately, there's an antidote. You can change your mindset to one that anticipates success.

With this mindset, you think of yourself as capable of handling the obstacles in your path, and you believe that you have the power to change your situation for the better. When you think like a child learning to walk, picking yourself up to take another step until it sticks, you'll forget that failure exists.

So, every day I encourage you to:

- Describe to yourself what you're doing well
- Frame ways to improve in a positive, proactive light
- Appreciate what you have right now

This is more difficult for some people than others. If that's true for you, you might be stuck on your loss, and caught in the trap of thinking "I just want to feel happy again".

So what is happiness anyway?

FIND REAL HAPPINESS

The Dalai Lama said the very purpose of life is to seek happiness. Where it gets confusing is pinpointing just what happiness means.

According to Russ Harris, one of the world's leading experts on positive psychology, most people have a flawed sense of happiness, for they believe that happiness is tied to pleasure. But, this kind of happiness is short-lived. Even when you keep doing or getting more of what initially made you happy, you can find happiness slips out of reach.[2]

It might be a case of having too much of a good thing, or simply that the pleasure has no meaning for you anymore. And if you try to pursue more of these good things, it can often lead you to the opposite effect.

Instead, Harris encourages us to realise that happiness is "living a rich and meaningful life." This type of happiness is profoundly tied to values and beliefs. It occurs when we take action that supports our view of these things.[3]

What must be expected, however, is to take the good with the bad. For a life lived in this way doesn't help you avoid uncomfortable feelings - that would

be unrealistic, and quite frankly, at odds with the human condition.

So, why am I bringing this up?

Russ Harris and other leaders in the field of positive psychology suggest that it's far more valuable to live with the idea that happiness means fulfilment rather than pleasure. That's why the purpose of this book is to help you identify a job that will enrich your life and help you achieve a sense of vitality moving forward.

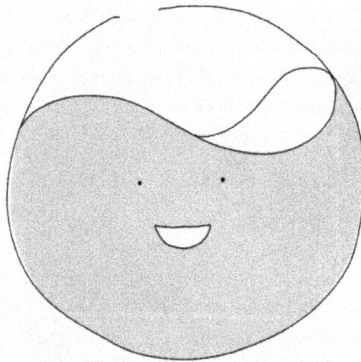

FILLED WITH FULFILMENT!

Of course, we all enjoy feeling good. We should certainly make the most of these feelings when they present, but we have to be realistic and know

that when we try to have them all the time, we're doomed to failure.

As you are no doubt discovering as a job seeker, rejection, crisis and disappointment are unavoidable facts of life.

But when your life is rooted in the realistic version of happiness, you'll find difficult feelings easier to bear when they show up next time. You can reduce the influence of pain and discover things to enjoy in life.

RESILIENT

Maintaining an optimistic mindset is like any other skill. You'll get the best results if you work at it every day. And right now is an especially crucial time to work on your own mental wellbeing. You've got a lot to deal with, a lot to consider, a lot to work through and a lot to do. You can't afford to get caught in the trap of destructive thinking.

According to Dr Martin Seligman, and 15 years of scientific research, there are two types of people in the world. Those who bounce back from failure and those who collapse.[4]

But the good news is, those prone to collapsing can build their resilience skills so that they too, can

experience growth after trauma.

Seligman's determination of the two "explanatory styles" that inform these outcomes are known as optimistic and pessimistic. According to the 3 Ps of resilience (permanence, pervasiveness and personalisation), optimism is when you interpret setbacks as "temporary, local and changeable (it's going away quickly, it's just this one situation, and I can do something about it)."[5]

On the other hand, pessimism is when setbacks are interpreted as "permanent, far-reaching and internal ("it's going to haunt me, impact every part of my life and I've only myself to blame").

The following action steps (defeat destructive thinking and the gratitude journal) are two simple ways to build more resilience by helping to reduce catastrophic thinking. Before you complete the action steps, take a pulse check and see how you describe your loss in relation to the 3 Ps of resilience.

ACTION STEPS

Describe your current job situation and see how it holds up against the 3Ps (permanence, pervasiveness and personalisation).

_____

_____

_____

_____

_____

_____

Defeat destructive thinking

List three pessimistic statements you've found yourself making in the past few days.

1. _____

_____

_____

2. _____

_____

_____

3. _____

_____

_____

ANTICIPATE SUCCESS

Now, for each of those statements, list three positive actions you can take to change the outcome.

1. _____
_____
_____

2. _____
_____
_____

3. _____
_____
_____

Gratitude journal

Every day, take 5 minutes to:

1. Describe to yourself what you're doing well.

_____
_____
_____
_____
_____
_____

2. Frame ways you can improve in a positive, proactive light.

_____
_____
_____
_____
_____
_____

3. Appreciate what you have now.

_____
_____
_____
_____
_____
_____

After completing the action steps every few days, take another pulse check and see if your view of your situation is improving according to the 3 Ps of resilience (permanence, pervasiveness and personalisation).

_____
_____
_____
_____
_____
_____

FACING DOWN THE SLAP

You already learned about the reality slap in Chapter 2. Now I want to introduce you to the concept coined by Russ Harris - the reality gap. The reality gap is the difference between where you are now and where you want to be. Sometimes in life, we can close a reality gap quickly, but at other times it's a much slower process, or even impossible to close. Even when you can't *close* the gap, there is no reason why you can't find fulfillment.[6]

That's what the aim of this book is. Consider that there might not be a quick fix to close that gap and fall into your dream job. That you might need to do some hard work and look inward. Figure out what's important to you, and how you could find enrichment in your career - even if that looks completely different from what you imagined, or the one that you had before.

Before you proceed further into the book, I'd like to ask you to do one thing: remain open.

The look of success doesn't always stay the same. For society, for an industry or you personally. So that you don't pass by any career opportunities that are outside the traditional model of employment, give

some thought to these two models of vocational development and challenge your career mindset to entertain more flexibility. [7]

The boundaryless career

OPTION 1

what you do want

→ boundaryless career

With this career model, you realise there is more to working life than the 3-box model of a traditional career trajectory: go to school, work and retire.

traditional career (what you DON'T want)

GO TO SCHOOL → WORK → RETIRE

You see different paths as a possibility for your life. If you're not fulfilled in a particular type of work or with a specific employee, you know it's acceptable

for you to move onto another. You seek work that is a better fit for your values and interests, rather than believing you owe your loyalty to just one employer.[8]

The self-directed career

OPTION 2 $\longrightarrow$ self - directed career

what you do want

The traditional career mindset can result in you feeling a lack of control over your own career - for the pathway is already set in stone. But with a more flexible and proactive mindset, you have a sense of self-direction. You feel the power to express your own values within your position, and this helps you feel intrinsically rewarded. When that happens, you feel a close tie between your work and your personal identity.[9]

ACCEPTANCE AND THE ROAD AHEAD

What will set you apart from others as you begin your job search, is how you respond to your situation. Proactivity and positivity are key, but you can't expect to replace negative feelings with positive ones.

A holistic approach to your life at this time is crucial. Instead of just focusing on a solution to the problem (i.e. finding a job), you should concentrate on yourself as a whole.

Here are some simple strategies to help you anticipate success and stay on a healthy life track.

(1) Do whatever it takes to feel strong and fit

That might include doing something special for your family, escaping on a camping trip in the great outdoors or continuing with your regular daily run. Whatever that looks like for *you* - do it. Physical resilience has a lot to do with mental and emotional resilience. No matter how much you want to, wallowing on the couch day after day just isn't going to help you feel any stronger.

(2) Surround yourself with positivity

The key to *not* wallowing is to avoid surrounding yourself with negative people. Misery loves company, and while you must accept your negative feelings, it's crucial those around you don't exacerbate them.

Instead, spend your time with those who have a positive influence on you.

(3) Extend kindness to others

This can be a time you're tempted to feel very selfish, and you do need to concentrate on yourself of course. But being helpful can go a long way to boost your attitude and help others see you in the right light. Who knows what will come your way. Offers from others, introductions or even the discovery of something you might like to pursue as a job.

(4) Fill your empty days with purposeful activity

Treat finding a job as your new job. During this time, it's important to set goals. But to boost your confidence and maintain patience, your goals should be based on action, rather than results. For example, "I will send out ten applications this week," rather than, "I will have a new job by the end of the month."

REMIND YOURSELF OF THE GOOD

At the end of the day, even though job loss is painful and career transitions may be hard work, there is a lot of good that can come from this time. For you are now presented with an opportunity:

- For self-discovery
- To upskill
- To embrace an attitude of lifelong learning
- To take control of the next phase of your life
- To find out what you'd like to do next
- To maximise the things that enrich your life and minimise those that deplete you
- To expand your network
- To set an example for your children on coping with setbacks

Much as it's in our nature to hold onto the negative, know that hidden beneath is the chance to be happy and lead a rich and fulfilled life. Keep this in mind as you proceed, and you'll start to see the opportunities opening up before you.

KEY LESSONS

As you anticipate success and move beyond the emotional ties of your job change, I encourage you to revisit these lessons from the chapter you just read.

Moving forward in the career direction of your choice will come much easier to you when you approach it with the right mindset.

- You need to stay future-focused to anticipate success
- You must understand the happiness in leading a rich and fulfilling life, rather than simply seeking pleasure
- You should develop resilience so that failure doesn't keep you down
- You must be flexible and open to seeking out opportunities

Finally, you should place great focus on self-care by:

- Doing things to stay strong and fit
- Surrounding yourself with positive people
- Being kind to others
- Seeking purposeful activity

Develop the right mindset, and you will be in a strong position to take control of the next phase of your life and figure out what you would like to do for work.

Chapter 4 provides you with the opportunity to uncover where your strengths lie, and start forming an idea of your ideal career direction.

CHAPTER 4

COMPETENCIES AS CLUES TO YOUR CAREER

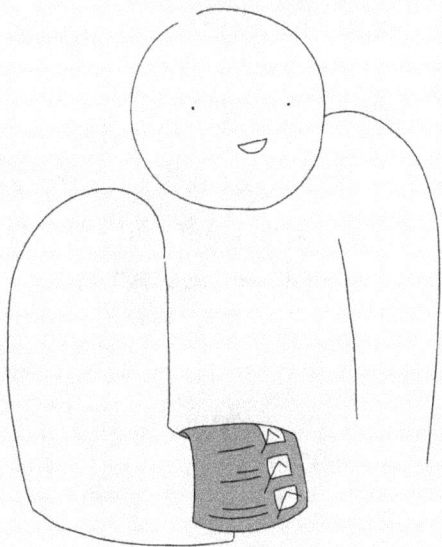

PART 2

Who are you?

In Part 1 of this book, I introduced you to the idea of happiness as a way to enrich your life, rather than find fleeting pleasure. But, how do you know which career direction will help you build that life of vitality?

If you believe you can predict your ideal job right now before any further consideration, you could be sorely mistaken.

"Research suggests that human beings are remarkably bad at predicting how they will feel when doing something in the future."[1]

Are you astonished to hear this?

Strangely, there is an upside. It may come as a relief to realise that any past job which worked out differently to how you expected may have been a result of this factor. After all, doing the thing is far different an experience from that of imagining yourself do it. So, if your imagination and your belief of what will make you happy aren't the ideal guides to choosing a career, what is?

Well, there are individual building blocks that have formed you as a person and your life so far. These building blocks will give you the clues to help you choose a career that you are suited to, by maximising those that enrich your life and minimising those that deplete your energy. I'm talking about the accomplishments, skills, interests, values, motivations and social core that you already hold.

Not only will these building blocks or clues help you determine your path forward, but they will also be eminently useful as you proceed into the world of job applications and interviews so you can present yourself in the best light.

Therefore in this chapter, we'll explore what your accomplishments and skills are, to help you hone in on a clear picture of yourself.

ASSESS YOUR COMPETENCE

Andy Grove said, "To understand a company's strategy, look at what they actually do rather than what they say they will do."[2] In the same way, the best means of directing your career is to look back on past indicators. What you have done in the past, namely your skills and accomplishments is an essential predictor of where your job can go.

In other words, now is the time to assess your competence.

According to Edward Deci and Richard Ryan's *Self-Determination Theory*, people seek out three things above all others: relatedness, competence and autonomy.[3] These three things are vital to look for in your new job.

Self determination theory

↓

RELATEDNESS
AUTONOMY
COMPETENCY

Why?

Having a job centred around your 'passion' isn't

enough to guarantee you'll find the work fulfilling. In fact, Cal Newport, author of *So Good They Can't Ignore You*, found that as people's confidence and experience in a job grows, so does their passion (not the other way around).

This point governs one of Newport's rules of figuring out what to do with your life - which you would be wise to keep in mind as you continue on your journey:

RULE #2: Be So Good They Can't Ignore You (Or, the Importance of Skill)".[4]

That's why this chapter focuses on identifying your accomplishments and skills so you may use them to your advantage in your job search.

The good news for those just starting out in your career is that this process doesn't exclude you. Consider this: accomplishments and skills are present in all aspects of life - not just a working environment. So, as you proceed through this chapter don't just think about "on the job" capabilities, but also those you've demonstrated in community-based activities, sports teams, group assignments during study and volunteer work too.

ACCOMPLISHMENTS

So, why is what we achieve so important?

For one thing, it's a question commonly asked in job interviews, where you're asked to provide an example of an achievement or accomplishment you're proud of. In these circumstances, we tend to rely on examples that don't necessarily mean the most to us but cast us in the best light for a particular position.

That's fine. But, our accomplishments also play an important role when you're figuring out who you are in order to determine your next career path. And for this purpose, achievements should take on a slightly different meaning. That is, you should be looking at things in your life that have given you a sense of satisfaction. These are the achievements that you feel have enriched your career or life.

According to Tom Morris, in *The Art of Achievement*, "The meaning of life is not to be found in having lots of money, fame, prestige, or stuff. It's to be found in living your proper quest of positive achievement. Make a difference in the lives of other people, make a difference for good, create new relationships, new feelings, new structures of goodness in the world by

what you do and who you are, and you will feel in that process what we so often seek with such futility in all the wrong places. The right sort of quest can be enjoyed at the deepest possible levels."[5]

While working is essential, what we accomplish in life extends far beyond that. When you take qualities that are not exclusive to work, like your values, interests and motivations, and connect them with your achievements within a career, that's when the magic really happens. Morris also encourages you to believe that accomplishment and enjoyment aren't mutually exclusive.[6]

Whether you're fresh out of school or a seasoned professional, know this: "to build confidence, build competence."[7] What's more, you need to be able to identify your competencies. Because when you can articulate your achievements to yourself and others, your confidence in your ability and the direction you choose will grow.

Uncovering your accomplishments

So, how do you figure out what your accomplishments are?

A great starting point is to look at what you have

achieved in your life so far. Accomplishments are things in your life that give a sense of genuine satisfaction. You'll probably have to do some real detective work to uncover these, but they are there - sometimes tucked away in the recesses of your mind and heart.

They could be things or events that you take little notice of because you think of them as normal or they came so easily that they're no big deal to you. They might be things that were downplayed by others, or maybe others couldn't understand why they meant something to you. That doesn't matter. You're not looking at your achievements right now through anyone else's eyes but your own. You shouldn't dismiss any of them, because they are huge clues to your life.

I find that when I coach job seekers who are just starting their careers, they falsely believe they haven't achieved anything yet. But, that's not really the case. You might have to dig deep to recognise them, but we all have achieved things. You shouldn't be hard on yourself and have unrealistically high standards.

Remember too, that accomplishments come in different forms. They might be goal-oriented or results-driven, value-driven, showcase experience level, demonstrate subject-matter knowledge or showcase your uniqueness.

So, I want you to look for clues of what you have accomplished or where you achieved consistently in your own life. Perhaps you felt good after running a marathon or successfully executing a complex recipe.

I teach people to document each of their accomplishments with a template:

(1) **The Situation: S** what was happening, something that needed fixing, the issue or an opportunity.

(2) **The Action: A** what did you do to fix the situation.

(3) **The Outcome: O** what made you feel good.

1. THE **S**ITUATION what was happening something that needed fixing the issue or an opportunity

2. THE **A**CTION what did you do to fix the situation

3. THE **O**UTCOME what made you feel good

If you're Australian, you probably grew up eating a certain favourite biscuit - the SAO. This can be a helpful way to remember situation, action and outcome.

When you are documenting the accomplishments you feel good about, I suggest that you look at four main areas of your life: **work, personal, educational, and volunteer or community.**

Before you start making your list, I suggest you read the following section to get you started.

Prompt for identifying your wins

If you're having trouble identifying the things you are most proud of achieving in your life, don't worry. Because you'll be wading through years of your life when identifying your accomplishments to date, you might find they don't all spring to mind at once. That's to be expected.

In fact, in order to get a clear picture of where you've excelled across the whole spectrum of your life, it's best to team self-reflection with some prompts. Here are some suggestions to guide you:

- What are your personal interests and hobbies? What went well for you?

- Do you have certificates or other physical evidence of your accomplishments?

- What are each of the roles you have held and what did you find the most personally satisfying about each one?

- Ask your colleagues or those you've done community-based activities with to see if they come up with a different set of achievements to you.

- Ask your friends and family what has stood out most to them or that you seemed most pleased by.

- Are there any stories you often tell that you are most proud of?

- Look over your social feeds and Facebook timeline for clues.

- If you've kept journals or diaries in the past - what gold nuggets of achievement do they contain?

- Look back through past photos, and you might be surprised by what you find - evidence of a successful fundraiser you contributed your time to? Gaining a black belt in Tae Kwon Do?

ask friends and family

personal interests

photos

your go to stories

Uncovering achievements

hobbies

Social feeds

certificates

journals

ask co-workers

Satisfying things from prior roles

Tip: If you'd like to keep better track of your accomplishments going forward, I suggest just 5-10 minutes of daily journaling or recording them regularly in a dedicated spreadsheet.

ACTION STEPS

1. Where possible for your circumstances, identify two achievements in each category:

- Work accomplishments

_____

_____

- Personal accomplishments

_____

_____

- Educational accomplishments

_____

_____

- Volunteer/communal accomplishments

_____

_____

2. Now, use the SAO template to look more closely at those achievements.

- **The Situation: S**. What was happening, something that needed fixing, the issue or an opportunity.

_____

_____

_____

- **The Action: A**. What did you do to fix the situation.

_____

_____

_____

- **The Outcome: O**. What made you feel good.

_____

_____

_____

Here's an example to get you started. If a personal achievement for you was losing weight, the SAO might look like this:

- The Situation: S. Over the years your weight gain had started to impact your health and your doctor said you needed to improve your lifestyle. You never played outside with your kids because you got out of breath so quickly.

- The Action: A. You started attending classes at your local gym regularly and improved your diet.

- The Outcome: O. It felt good to make positive changes in your life and see the results - both in your health and your appearance. You don't make excuses for not playing outside with your young children anymore - because you feel fit enough to join in.

Once you have identified your top 8 accomplishments, it's time to look at your skills.

SKILLS

To get this going, you'll be breaking down each accomplishment by the types of skills you used in achieving them. But first, you need to have a good understanding of what skills really are.

A skill is your ability to do something. Like your achievements, skills aren't just learned on the job. In fact, any part of your life can help you develop skills.

Every person is unique. If you are going to make a success of your career, there are key skills you already possess that you can use as leverage points.

Let's look at what they are and how to find them.

Skills fall under two umbrellas: hard skills and soft skills.

Hard skills vs. soft skills

Hard: These types of skills are tangible, easily defined and verifiable.

Take the example of golf. Being able to play golf well (or even adequately) is a hard skill - we can see it demonstrated right in front of us.

Hard skills can be either functional or formal. More on this in a moment.[8]

Soft: These types of skills are intangible, that is, you can't see them at play. Rather, you get a sense of them. If someone said, "you're a great listener" that is the perfect example of a soft skill.

Soft skills are also known as personality skills. More on these in a moment.[9]

In the past, hard skills were most valued by employers. After all, they can be more clearly demonstrated and are easy to list on a resume. This employment style is centred around the attitude of "getting the job done." But, what about how the job is done and what it means for the success of the company and the individual, one year, five or even ten years from now?

This is precisely why soft skills are starting to rise in importance in the eyes of employers. In fact, a Manpower survey of 2,000 US employers showed "61% of American companies rated such *soft* abilities as communication, collaboration and problem-solving as the most desired skills in prospective hires."[10]

of american companies rated such "soft" abilities as communication, collaboration and problem solving as the most desired skills in prospective hires

With the changing nature of the workforce today, these skills are essential.

This brings us to the idea of emotional intelligence (EQ) now being more important than traditional intelligence (IQ).

Why EQ is front of mind

Much like hard skills were traditionally favoured in the workplace, so was IQ. But today, evidence is showing that EQ is actually more important than IQ. "In fact, some research states that emotional intelligence is responsible for 58% of your job performance and that 90% of top performers have high EQ."[11]

EQ is related to your soft skills and can be improved on over time.[12]
It is generally considered to encompass abilities like being:

- Self-aware
- Self-managing
- Self-regulating
- Self-motivating
- Empathic[13]

These are highly-desired traits, so when you are identifying the skills you already possess, I want you to ensure you don't discount those "softer" skills that portray emotional intelligence.

Now, let's look at the three specific types of skills you have.

FUNCTIONAL, FORMAL AND PERSONALITY SKILLS

Functional skills

These are the skills associated with people, data or things. These types of skills are thought of as transferable because you can apply them to many tasks or work settings. For example:

- Writing
- Numeracy
- Record keeping
- Research
- Prioritising

Formal skills

These are knowledge-based, job-specific skills or those you've gained competency in via the education system. These skills are the least transferable and not as easily applied in other environments or situations. For example:

- How to perform a tax return in accounting
- How to use checkout software for a major supermarket
- How to conduct a drone-survey of a road

Personality skills

These are the patterns of behaviour that come naturally to you. They are your soft or human skills such as:

- Reliability
- Adaptability
- Motivation
- Rationality
- Diplomacy

Tip: use the following skills lists to guide you as you complete the action steps.

Functional skills

Achieve

Acquire

Adapt

Adjust

Administer

Advocate

Analyze

Analyze Data

Analyze Ideas

Anticipate Consequences

Anticipate Problems

Apply Policy

Arrange

Ask Questions

Assemble

Assume Responsibility

Attend to Details

Brainstorm New Ideas

Build

Buy

Calculate / Compare

Categorize

Clarify

Classify

Coach

Communicate

Compare

Compile

Compose

Conceptualize

Conduct
Construct
Consult
Conversational Ability
Coordinate
Counsel
Create
Create Images
Critical Thinking
Deal with Public
Debate
Decide
Define
Delegate
Design
Design Programs
Determine Policy
Develop
Develop Systems
Develop Theory
Direct
Display
Edit
Empathize
Encourage
Enlist'
Entertain, Perform
Establish
Evaluate
Examine
Execute
Expand
Expedite
Explain
Facilitate
Facilitate Discussion
Finalize
Forecast
Formulate Hypotheses

Foster
Gather Data
Generate
Give Directions
Group Process
Handle Logistics
Help
Hire
Host
Implement
Improve
Improvise
Increase
Influence
Inform
Initiate
Initiate Projects
Install
Instruct
Interpersonal Skills
Interpret
Interpret Policy
Interview
Interview for Information
Invent
Investigate
Keep Records
Launch
Layout/Format
Lead
Listen
Logical Ability
Maintain
Make Decisions
Make Presentations
Manage
Manage Information
Math Skills
Mediate

COMPETENCIES AS CLUES TO YOUR CAREER

Meet Deadlines
Memorize
Monitor
Motivate
Negotiate
Observe
Operate Equipment
Organize
Organize Information
Outline
Perceive
Perform
Persuade
Plan
Prepare
Present
Prioritize
Program
Promote
Prove
Provide Care
Public Speaking
Put Theory into Practice
Question
Read for Information
Recommend
Reconcile
Recruit
Renovate
Repair

Report
Research
Resolve Conflicts
Restore
Review
Revise
Schedule
Select
Sell
Sensitivity to Needs
Set Priorities
Solve Problems
Stimulate
Strategize
Streamline Systems
Summarize
Supervise
Synthesize Information
Teach
Teamwork
Think on One's Feet
Think Visually
Time Management
Train
Translate
Use Intuition
Use Languages
Use Physical Coordination
Verbal Communication
Write

Personality skills

Accurate
Adaptable
Add Value
Adventurous

Aggressive
Alert
Ambitious
Amiable

Analytical
Argumentative
Articulate
Assertive
Attentive
Broad-minded
Businesslike
Calm
Capable
Careful
Caring
Cautious
Competent
Competitive
Confident
Conscientious
Consistent
Cooperative
Courageous
Creative
Curious
Decisive
Dedicated
Dependable
Determined
Easygoing
Efficient
Empathetic
Energetic
Enterprising
Enthusiastic
Firm
Flexible
Fun
Fussy
Hardworking
Honest
Humorous
Idealistic

Imaginative
Independent
Industrious
Innovative
Inspiring
Intuitive
Inventive
Kind
Loyal
Moody
Motivated
Opportunistic
Optimistic
Organized
Patient
People-oriented
Persevering
Persistent
Practical
Praising
Productive
Realistic
Relaxed
Reliable
Resourceful
Responsible
Risk Taker
Serious
Sociable
Spendthrift
Systematic
Tactful
Talkative
Thoughtful
Tolerant
Tough
Trusting
Versatile

ACTION STEPS

- Identify the skills that were paramount to your eight achievements and mark whether these were functional, formal or personality skills. Ideally, you'll find that you used some skills multiple times.

_____

_____

_____

_____

_____

- Tally how many times you used each skill

_____

_____

_____

_____

- Now, looking at your list of skills and their tallies, identify your top 5 skills (i.e. those skills you used most) for each of the three skill types.

Top 5 functional skills

_____

_____

_____

_____

_____

Top 5 formal skills

_____
_____
_____
_____
_____

Top 5 personality skills

_____
_____
_____
_____
_____

These are your core skills. Once you can see how your skills are ranked, your achievements will be much easier to understand. And you'll also be able to clearly see the skills you already possess which will provide clues to your future career direction.

Discover your strengths

Another way of understanding your personality skills is to refer to the work on character strengths done by the VIA Institute. They define character strengths as innate, but able to be honed so you can reach peak performance.[14]

You can find out what your signature strengths are (those most essential to who you are) by taking the VIA strengths-finding survey. Research has shown that when you undertake work that allows you to use your signature strengths, you receive greater pleasure, job satisfaction, engagement and meaning.[15]

ACTION STEPS

VIA strengths-finding survey

1. Register an account online at http://www.viacharacter.org/Survey/Account/Register.

2. Now, you will be directed to answer 120 questions about yourself.

3. Upon completing the 120 questions, you will receive a report which details 24 Signature Strengths from most dominant (no. 1) to least dominant (no. 24).

4. Look at your 10 most dominant signature strengths from the survey. What clues do your signature strengths give you about a possible career path?

_____
_____
_____
_____
_____

WHY PEOPLE FAIL

According to Siimon Reynolds, author of *Why People Fail*, there are 16 obstacles to success.[16] Incredibly, these all stem from within ourselves and in essence, they drill down to either our bad habits or self-doubt. Even when you've developed a great mindset, it can be easy to slip back and let one or more of the 16 obstacles cloud your judgement when you're exploring options or making decisions about your future career.

14 lack of persistence

1 unclear purpose   9 poor self

16 not focusing on   2 destructive thinking   image
strengths

3 low productivity   4 fixed mindset
                                                    12 stress
OBSTACLES

5 weak energy   7 poor presentation skills

6 not asking the right questions   11 no daily
                                                    rituals
8 mistaking IQ for EQ   10 not enough thinking

13 few relationships   15 money
                                            obsession

When that happens, I suggest you refer back to this chapter. Nothing can give you a boost of confidence like reminding yourself of your history of achievements and the skills that helped you get there.

KEY LESSONS

As you begin to formulate how your accomplishments and skills (or competency) can guide you forward, I encourage you to revisit these lessons from the chapter you just read.

Cal Newport proposes four rules for choosing what you'd like to do for work. I want you to remember this one in particular:

- "Be so good they can't ignore you"[17]

Your achievements and skills are among your biggest advantages in your job search - whether that's in terms of beating out your competition or determining a potential career path.

Accomplishments are the things in your life that have given you a sense of satisfaction. They come from your work life, but your personal life too. When you accomplish things, you don't only satisfy your innate need for competence; you're building confidence as well - a desirable trait.

The SAO template is useful for documenting and understanding achievements by considering:

- The **S**ituation
- The **A**ction
- The **O**utcome

Your skills are what you relied on to achieve these accomplishments. There are three types of skills:

- Functional
- Formal
- Personality

Identifying your core skills gives you greater insight into your accomplishments, but also gives you more of those vital clues to guide you in your job search.

Don't forget to refer back to your lists of accomplishments and skills to remind yourself of your competence if any moments of self-doubt creep in.

Chapter 5 brings you to the next clue in identifying your enriched career: your interests.

CHAPTER 5

WHERE DO YOU GET LOST?

PART 2

Who are you?

Everyone wants the opportunity to "do what they love." Unfortunately, not everyone believes this is possible. What would it mean to you, if I told you that it's not only possible, that it's recommended?

Would it excite you to learn that:

- You could get out of bed and look forward to going to work?
- You could find enjoyment and fulfilment in expressing parts of your authentic self, at work?
- You could enjoy more power in your career, just by incorporating aspects of what you love?

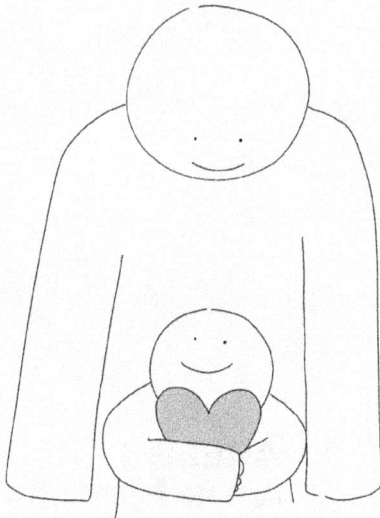

I'm going to show you how this is indeed possible.

In the previous chapter, you discovered what you

are good at, so now it's time to consider what you love doing.

What makes you come alive?

What fires you up?

What do you never want to put down, once you pick it up?

These are your interests. Those things that you get so lost in, that times runs away from you.

Your interests are an essential component of what makes you, you. In fact, you use them to make many decisions about your life already:

- How you spend free time
- Who you spend time with
- Where you spend your time

So, it's reasonable to conclude that interests should also play a role in informing your ideal career.

BENEFITS OF A CAREER THAT INCORPORATES YOUR INTERESTS

There are three primary reasons you should pursue a career which includes your interests:

WHERE DO YOU GET LOST?

① Boosts your commitment and engagement

In a work sense, if you are interested in something, then you are going to be much more committed to it. That's why it's essential you find a job that includes your interests in some form.

It's quite common for people to find themselves in jobs in which they perform very well, but at some point boredom sets in. When there isn't a correlation between your interests and your job, then your engagement suffers, you'll find it hard to get excited about new products or services, and you'll have trouble seeing a future with that employer.

② Work is no longer a chore

While to others, a certain career may look like a chore, most of the time it won't even seem like work to you. That's because interests are unique to you - particularly when your chosen career isn't just based on your interests, but also your strengths.

③ Gives you unique power

When your career is a fit with your authentic self, you can't help but stand out. A job that reflects your interests gives you more opportunity to express yourself through your work and others will notice that. You'll be in the enviable position of being seen as "uniquely capable and uniquely powerful."[1]

HOW TO DRAW OUT YOUR INTERESTS

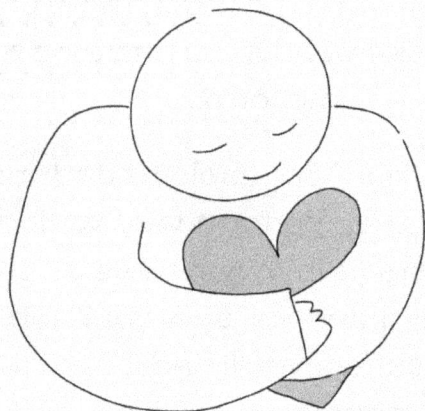

Before you start to pinpoint your interests, I want to emphasise that there is no one right answer. And more importantly - that you should not be concerned with what you (or others) believe your interests should be, only what they authentically are.

To start thinking deeply about what your interests are, I suggest you work your way through the following list of questions first. In effect, you need to be your own personal coach and undertake a process of self-questioning.

Even though the end-goal is the same as asking *what are my interests*, by asking specific, pointed questions, you will elicit more insightful answers.

They may even surprise you.

The following questions are designed to prompt your realisation of what you love, from the most obvious, to those you've perhaps forgotten throughout your life so far.

The most important part of this process is to *write down your answers*. That way you won't lose any gems, and you can read back over them to get a well-rounded view of just what it is that you love.

ACTION STEPS

1. What hobbies did you do before life got so busy? Would you like to take up any of them again?

_____

_____

_____

_____

_____

_____

2. What topic could you read 200 books about and still want to know more?

_____
_____
_____
_____
_____
_____

3. Thinking about your current or past jobs, what activities or tasks did you find the most engaging?

_____
_____
_____
_____
_____
_____

4. If money wasn't a consideration, what would you happily do for the next five years, without pay?

_____
_____
_____
_____
_____
_____

5. Imagine you have retired from work. What do you wish you had done with your time in the last 20 years?

_____

_____

_____

_____

_____

6. What activities and subjects did you enjoy throughout your studies? Do these still hold a level of interest for you? Is there one you would be happy to re-engage with?

_____

_____

_____

_____

_____

7. Ask those closest to you - what do you seem to do the most enthusiastically?

_____

_____

_____

_____

_____

8. What did you enjoy during your childhood, before external pressures set in, like getting good grades or finding a good job?

_____

_____

_____

_____

_____

9. If you could finish your working day one hour earlier, every day, how would you spend your time? What would you be most excited to do?

_____

_____

_____

_____

_____

10. What childhood dream did you hold, that you didn't have the opportunity to explore fully? Does it still intrigue you?

_____

_____

_____

_____

_____

11. If you had the financial freedom to do anything, what would you spend your time doing?

_____

_____

_____

_____

_____

_____

12. Drawing on your answers from Chapter 4, what skills do you have that you also really love to do?

_____

_____

_____

_____

_____

13. What burning desire do you hold, that you would like to achieve before you die?

_____

_____

_____

_____

_____

14. In detail, describe what your ideal day would look like?

_____
_____
_____
_____
_____
_____

15. Is there someone who really inspires you? Why is that, and what can you learn from them?

_____
_____
_____
_____
_____
_____

16. What do you enjoy doing, that despite setbacks, keeps you coming back for more?

_____
_____
_____
_____
_____
_____

WHAT ARE *YOUR* INTERESTS?

When it comes to analysing your interests and understanding just why they appeal to you, it's helpful to look across three categories:

- **People interests:** these are interests that allow for interaction or communication with others. In other words, they have a social aspect to them.

- **Informational interests:** these are the interests that may require you to learn or strategise. In some way, they challenge your thinking processes.

- **Object interests:** rather than focusing on the thinking or socialising aspects of an interest, you appreciate the look or experience it provides you.

You want to identify the one reason, in particular, each interest appeals to you.

Let's look at a concrete example to help you better understand your own interests.

Interest: golf

If you mainly likely to play golf because you like being with friends, that is a *people interest*.

OR If you are most interested in an analytical challenge of choosing the right golf club, or the strategy of the game, that indicates an *informational interest*.

OR If you play experiencing the beauty of getting to walk around the golf course, that is an *object interest*.

ACTION STEPS

You can use your answers to the previous set of questions as prompts for answering these, and of course, adding in any other interests that warrant a place here.

1. People Interests:

- Make a list of at least five interests that you enjoy doing with people.

_____

_____

_____

_____

_____

_____

- Is there something these activities all have in common?

_____

_____

_____

_____

_____

2. Informational Interests:

- Make a list of at least five interests that you enjoy doing with information or knowledge.

_____

_____

_____

_____

_____

_____

- Is there something these activities all have in common?

_____

_____

_____

_____

_____

_____

3. Object Interests:

- Make a list of at least five interests that you enjoy doing for the experience.

_____

_____

_____

_____

_____

_____

- Is there something these activities all have in common?

_____
_____
_____
_____
_____
_____

4. Now rank the interests and identify your top type of interest. This indicates your top core interest. This doesn't mean that you're not interested in other areas, just that one or two are your absolute focus. This is the interest area (people, informational or object) that you should ensure is a major part of your job.

_____
_____
_____
_____
_____
_____

STAY OPEN

When you have identified the patterns in your answers, you might start jumping to conclusions and letting past assumptions or beliefs about career choice stop you before you're even out of the gate.

Just because you might not see how your core interest holds potential for a future career now, doesn't make that true. It's too early to see how all the pieces fit together.

For now, I just ask you to remain open to the idea that your interests should play a role in your enriched career. There are a couple of strategies to help you do this.

(1) **Invest more time engaging with your interests**

If there are one or two in particular that you'd like to take up again or get more involved with, then find ways to do just that. You could volunteer, pick up a side gig or even find a mentor to learn more about that particular area.

(2) **Embrace a growth mindset of interest**

According to O'Keefe, Dweck and Walton, those with a growth mindset of interest believe "that interests can be developed and that, with commitment and investment, they can grow over time".[2]

What this means in the context of a career, is that a growth mindset of interest can help you create connections across multiple fields so that you are capable of innovative thought, fusing different areas into one novel idea and being more resilient to setbacks in your work. To broaden your own range of interests, you could consider experimenting with the hobbies that friends or family have, that have always intrigued you.

And remember, that the point of this exercise isn't to say that because your main interest is writing or painting, you can only become an author or an artist - that mode of career planning is far too restrictive. This is just one building block of your life that will help you discover your path to your future enriched career.

KEY LESSONS

As you reflect on what's important to you, I encourage you to revisit these lessons from the chapter you just read.

While some may say it's too idealistic to believe that everyone can "do what they love", I firmly believe that your interests are one of the key components to an enriched career.

In a work sense, if you are interested in something, you will be more engaged with the work, and therefore, more committed to your role, and your employer.

When your career incorporates your interests, you will also find yourself harnessing more capability and power than you ever believed possible.

To identify your interests, you should explore the three types, known as people, informational and object interests. Clues to these not only lie in how you spend your time now, but are also found in what you loved in the past, and either didn't have the chance to explore, or left behind as your life became preoccupied with other things.

It's crucial you understand yourself and the building blocks that make up who you are if you are to move into a job that brings vitality to your life.

When it comes to analysing your interests, you may find that some of them are driven by what you value. We'll look at values next, in Chapter 6, along with motivations and your social core.

CHAPTER 6

WHAT'S IMPORTANT TO YOU?

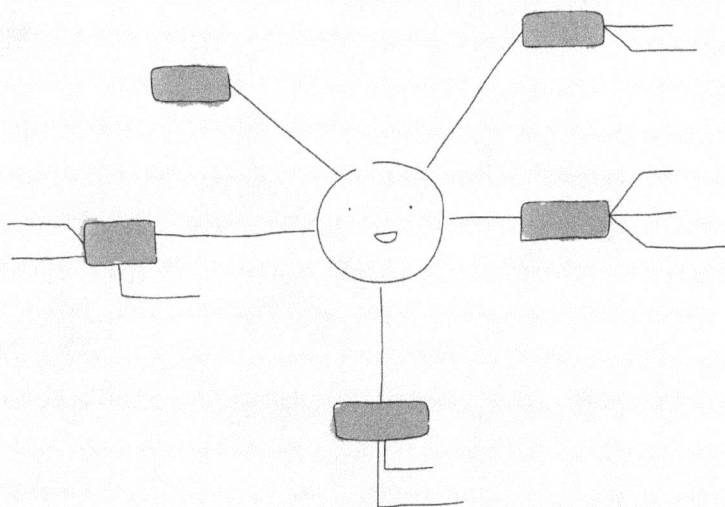

PART 2

Who are you?

When you're moving into a new job, you're probably thinking about whether it's a job you can do, you want to do, and of course, the clincher - if they want you. But, there's one thought that might be getting pushed to the back of your mind. And that is whether *you'll fit in*.

You see, employees join companies for the *opportunity*. But, they often leave them because of the people or *culture*. This tells us that feeling comfortable with the people you're going to be working with and what they represent, isn't a luxury - it's essential to your happiness in your chosen career.

Luckily, like the other aspects you've explored so far in Part 2 of this book, you can uncover clues in your past to help you find a job where you'll feel most at home.

As you proceed through this chapter, you'll explore:

- Your own values and the need for shared values to exist within the workplace culture
- What motivates you and how that impacts what's important to you in a workplace and career
- Why workplace relationships are so significant, and why our people choices are often wrong
- Our innate need for relatedness and how it enriches life
- The proven approach to determine the traits of people you are most comfortable with or your social core
- How to tell if the people in your new workplace have these traits before you start

IMPORTANCE OF VALUES ALIGNMENT

Your values are what are most important to you. They are what you stand for, what you represent.

Values are always present, but unless we actively devote thought to them, we may not be entirely clear on what they are. If you aren't aware of what's important to you, it will be unclear which is the best road to take.

That applies to all decisions you'll make in your life - not just what you choose to do for work. However, values are handy filters for evaluating job opportunities and the organisational culture of a new employer.

Let's look at an obvious example.

If you are a vegan and are passionate about animal rights, it's clear that a career as a butcher or working for a company that tests its products on animals would be a poor choice for you. After all, there's a misalignment in values.

Similarly, if you are pro-gun control and, as a PR consultant, you have the opportunity to work for a political party that advocates for pro-gun measures, that is a poor fit with your values too.

The good news is you can learn how to become crystal-clear about your values so that you can identify the career opportunities that stack up positively and those you should walk away from. We are already subconsciously influenced by our values and tend to do whatever we place a value on. But, when it comes to a more complicated decision - like what to do for a career, it helps to put your values front and centre.

Understanding *your* values

Rather than undertake the daunting task of compiling your values from scratch, I suggest referring to Steve Pavlina's list of 400 values.[1] As you read through, you can circle the values that mean something to you. You can also access it here if you prefer: https://www.stevepavlina.com/blog/2004/11/list-of-values/

Abundance	Assertiveness	Chastity
Acceptance	Assurance	Cheerfulness
Accessibility	Attentiveness	Clarity
Accomplishment	Attractiveness	Cleanliness
Accountability	Audacity	Clear-mindedness
Accuracy	Availability	Cleverness
Achievement	Awareness	Closeness
Acknowledgement	Awe	Comfort
Activeness	Balance	Commitment
Adaptability	Beauty	Community
Adoration	Being the best	Compassion
Adroitness	Belonging	Competence
Advancement	Benevolence	Competition
Adventure	Bliss	Completion
Affection	Boldness	Composure
Affluence	Bravery	Concentration
Aggressiveness	Brilliance	Confidence
Agility	Buoyancy	Conformity
Alertness	Calmness	Delight
Altruism	Camaraderie	Dependability
Amazement	Candor	Depth
Ambition	Capability	Desire
Amusement	Care	Determination
Anticipation	Carefulness	Devotion
Appreciation	Celebrity	Devoutness
Approachability	Certainty	Dexterity
Approval	Challenge	Dignity
Art	Change	Diligence
Articulacy	Charity	Direction
Artistry	Charm	Directness

WHAT'S IMPORTANT TO YOU?

Discipline	Fascination	Imagination
Discovery	Fashion	Impact
Discretion	Fearlessness	Impartiality
Diversity	Ferocity	Independence
Dominance	Fidelity	Individuality
Dreaming	Fierceness	Industry
Drive	Financial indepen-	Influence
Duty	dence	Ingenuity
Dynamism	Firmness	Inquisitiveness
Eagerness	Fitness	Insightfulness
Ease	Flexibility	Inspiration
Economy	Flow	Integrity
Ecstasy	Fluency	Intellect
Education	Focus	Intelligence
Effectiveness	Fortitude	Intensity
Efficiency	Frankness	Intimacy
Elation	Freedom	Intrepidness
Elegance	Friendliness	Introspection
Empathy	Friendship	Introversion
Encouragement	Frugality	Intuition
Endurance	Fun	Intuitiveness
Energy	Gallantry	Inventiveness
Enjoyment	Generosity	Investing
Entertainment	Gentility	Involvement
Enthusiasm	Giving	Joy
Environmentalism	Grace	Judiciousness
Ethics	Gratitude	Justice
Euphoria	Gregariousness	Keenness
Excellence	Growth	Kindness
Excitement	Guidance	Knowledge
Exhilaration	Happiness	Leadership
Expectancy	Harmony	Learning
Expediency	Health	Liberation
Experience	Heart	Liberty
Expertise	Helpfulness	Lightness
Exploration	Heroism	Liveliness
Expressiveness	Holiness	Logic
Extravagance	Honesty	Longevity
Extroversion	Honor	Love
Exuberance	Hopefulness	Loyalty
Fairness	Hospitality	Majesty
Faith	Humility	Making a difference
Fame	Humor	Marriage
Family	Hygiene	Mastery

Maturity
Meaning
Meekness
Mellowness
Meticulousness
Mindfulness
Modesty
Motivation
Mysteriousness
Nature
Neatness
Nerve
Nonconformity
Obedience
Open-mindedness
Openness
Optimism
Order
Organization
Originality
Outdoors
Outlandishness
Outrageousness
Partnership
Patience
Passion
Peace
Perceptiveness
Perfection
Perkiness
Perseverance
Persistence
Persuasiveness
Philanthropy
Piety
Playfulness
Pleasantness
Pleasure
Poise
Polish
Popularity
Potency
Power
Practicality

Pragmatism
Precision
Preparedness
Presence
Pride
Privacy
Proactivity
Professionalism
Prosperity
Prudence
Punctuality
Purity
Rationality
Realism
Reason
Reasonableness
Recognition
Recreation
Refinement
Reflection
Relaxation
Reliability
Relief
Religiousness
Reputation
Resilience
Resolution
Resolve
Resourcefulness
Respect
Responsibility
Rest
Restraint
Reverence
Richness
Rigor
Sacredness
Sacrifice
Sagacity
Saintliness
Sanguinity
Satisfaction
Science
Security

Self-control
Selflessness
Self-reliance
Self-respect
Sensitivity
Sensuality
Serenity
Service
Sexiness
Sexuality
Sharing
Shrewdness
Significance
Silence
Silliness
Simplicity
Sincerity
Skillfulness
Solidarity
Solitude
Sophistication
Soundness
Speed
Spirit
Spirituality
Spontaneity
Spunk
Stability
Status
Stealth
Stillness
Strength
Structure
Success
Support
Supremacy
Surprise
Sympathy
Synergy
Teaching
Teamwork
Temperance
Thankfulness
Thoroughness

WHAT'S IMPORTANT TO YOU?

Thoughtfulness
Thrift
Tidiness
Timeliness
Traditionalism
Tranquility
Transcendence
Trust
Trustworthiness
Truth
Understanding
Unflappability
Uniqueness

Unity
Usefulness
Utility
Valor
Variety
Victory
Vigor
Virtue
Vision
Vitality
Vivacity
Volunteering
Warmheartedness

Warmth
Watchfulness
Wealth
Willfulness
Willingness
Winning
Wisdom
Wittiness
Wonder
Worthiness
Youthfulness
Zeal

ACTION STEPS

1. Choose your contenders

Start by reading through the entire list, circling each value that means something to you. Ideally, you should come up with a list of 30-40 values at this point.

2. Narrow it down

Now it's time to finetune it. Narrow your list down to a more manageable 5-7 values that you would prioritise above all others. If you find you have two or three values that are nearly identical, try to just choose one as a representative.

3. Define your values

Once you have your shortlist, it's time to create your own definition for each value. This is an important step because one value can mean different things to different people.

For example, the value of 'Giving' could be defined as the act of providing charity to worthy causes or those less fortunate; whereas another person might think Giving means being supportive, devoted or kind.

4. Come up with *at least one behaviour* that helps make it clear to you when each value is being expressed

The main point is to define whatever your value means to *you*.

For example, if you value 'Appreciation' then the related behaviour might be: to thank those who help you or those who go the extra mile with a given task.

Value:

_____

Definition of that value:

_____

Behaviours that underpin this value for you:

_____

_____

_____

_____

_____

_____

Now, what you have just learned about yourself will form a guide so that you continue on the right path to your ideal job, rather than pursuing one that is misaligned with your core values.

WHERE DO YOUR MOTIVATIONS LIE?

When you understand your inner-most motivations, it becomes more apparent where your strengths and weaknesses lie, and therefore what makes you feel most comfortable and fulfilled. This applies to your work, but also other essential domains in your life, like relationships and parenting.

For this book, and of course, your job search, you'll be looking at your own motivations in terms of how they relate to work. When your motivations are a natural fit with your work, research shows that you will not only perform better but have higher levels of appreciation for it and engagement too.

According to Heidi Grant and E. Tory Higgins, there are two types of motivations: promotion and prevention.[2] Although you might relate to elements of both (which is natural), one of these motivational types should appear dominant to you.

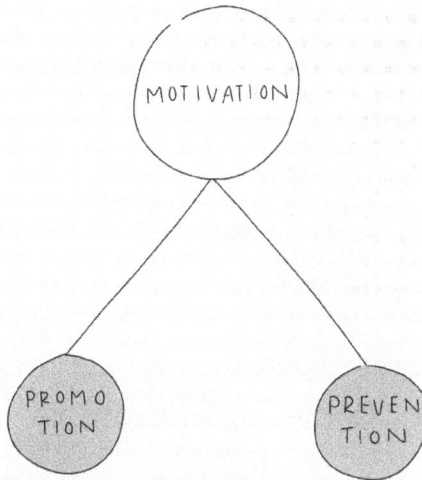

Promotion (playing to win)

Do you seek out opportunities for advancement or achievement? Then you might primarily be motivated by promotion, a desire to succeed and receive gains for achieving your goals.

Roles that will give you the opportunity for growth, creative thinking or the chance to work in a fast-paced industry could be an excellent fit for you.

"Promotion-focused people excel at:

- Creativity and innovation
- Seizing opportunities to get ahead
- Embracing risk
- Working quickly
- Generating lots of options and alternatives
- Abstract thinking"[3]

You may be suited to less practical and more creative types of work. Consider, for example:

- Social media
- Tech
- Consultative roles

When approaching a big change in your career, if you are promotion-focused you might have a more optimistic outlook than your prevention-focused colleagues. As such, you may be more willing to dive in and embrace it. However, the challenge is making sure you think through your decision - as you may be more prone to error and have a tendency to be unprepared with a plan B.

Prevention (playing NOT to lose)

Do you prefer to play defence and look for ways to hold onto everything you've worked so hard for?

Then you might primarily be motivated by prevention, a desire to be counted on, keeping things running like clockwork and above all, avoid any danger.

Roles that will provide you with stability, rules, and require a keen sense of detail could be a great fit for you.

"Prevention-focused people excel at:

- Thoroughness and being detail-oriented
- Analytical thinking and reasoning
- Planning
- Accuracy (working flawlessly)
- Reliability
- Anticipating problems"[4]

You may be suited to more practical and conventional types of work. Consider, for example:

- Administrative work
- Highly-technical work
- Contract law

When approaching a change in your career, a prevention-focused person might have a more pessimistic and cautious outlook than their promotion-minded colleagues. As such, they may be more hesitant to proceed with a life-changing decision. The upside for them is that the decision they do eventually make will be more carefully-considered and also have a plan B up their sleeve. [5]

I'm not saying that if you are prevention-motivated, you must work in contract law and that's that. This isn't a shortcut or one-size fits all solution. However, your motivations form part of the whole that makes you up as a person.

When you understand yourself from each of the perspectives we discuss, you have a better chance of seeing a career path for what it is, whether it aligns with what is important to you … and ultimately, whether it will be a good fit.

ACTION STEPS

1. Do you play to win or play NOT to lose? Decide whether you identify more with a promotion or prevention focus.

_____

_____

_____

_____

_____

_____

2. Can you think of some possible lines of work for you that fit with this focus?

_____

_____

_____

_____

_____

OUR INNATE NEED FOR RELATEDNESS

Finding where you fit isn't just a desire. As a human, this is also a basic need. Previously I introduced you to Edward Deci and Richard Ryan's *Self-Determination Theory*, which proposed that people seek out three things above all others: relatedness, competence and autonomy.[6] For the purpose of this chapter, we're going to look at the first factor: relatedness.

What is relatedness?

It's your need to feel connected to others and have them feel connected to you in return. It's also about feeling as though you're contributing to something greater than yourself.

Relatedness is the antidote to loneliness - that part of the human condition we try so hard to escape. It's why we surround ourselves with friends who are in intimate relationships and join clubs or groups with like-minded people. And, as Heidi Grant points out, "there doesn't seem to be such a thing as 'too much relatedness' - we can always benefit from new or deeper connections, from a greater sense of belonging."[7]

In fact, relatedness isn't only a desire; it's also vital to success in the workplace. And herein lies the premise of Claudio Fernández-Aráoz's book and its title: *It's Not the How or the What But the Who*.

Just look at Jeff Bezos and the success of Amazon. Bezos believes his talent pool should be ever-improving. To the point where "he'd rather interview fifty people and not hire anyone than hire the wrong person."[8] That's how important the who is to him.

What can you learn from this?

Even when you're not running one of the top companies in the world, surrounding yourself with the right people is essential to your success. That's not just about who is the best on paper, but how you will be able to work alongside people you respect every day.

When there are threats or failures of relatedness in the workplace, your engagement and your

performance will ultimately suffer. But, relatedness successes can mean you experience:

- Greater motivation
- Greater interest and enjoyment
- Better performance
- Feeling as though your voice is heard and respected
- Having opportunities to help others
- Feeling as though you're in an environment of trust

In fact, relatedness is a signifier of emotional intelligence (EQ). Naturalhr.com describes it as "encompassing our ability to build and maintain relationships, network, lead, manage conflict and work with others."[9] Not only does it satisfy one of your needs, it also makes you more valuable in the eyes of your employer.

It's clear why relatedness plays such a significant role in enriching your career, and therefore, your life.

Our people choices are often wrong

SYSTEM1 SYSTEM2

- Thinking fast
- Automatic
- not suited for people choices

- Thinking slow
- analytical
- well suited for people choices

According to Princeton economist Daniel Kahneman, when we need to make decisions or judgements, we have two systems of thinking that are at our disposal.[10] "System 1", is an automatic way of thinking, where we "place too much weight on the information in front of us, without stopping to ask what else we need to know in order to make sound assessments and accurate predictions."[11] This system is also called "Thinking Fast".

"System 2", or "Thinking Slow" is a controlled way of thinking. It is responsible for reasoning and problem-solving, by a focused, rational and analytical approach.[12]

Unfortunately, we often rely on the wrong system of thinking for the situation facing us - System 1. When we make System 1 decisions, we are effectively making snap, often error-prone judgements." This mode of thought is innate - instilled in us by our ancestors who were only required to decide whether they would fight, flee or partner with a stranger to meet a primitive goal of survival.

Your ancestors were able to make fast decisions, based purely on whether the stranger looked familiar or similar to them. That worked well for them. We're still hardwired to do this, but this mode of thought no longer serves us in the same way.

This tendency is present right from birth. A study demonstrated that babies recognise and show a preference for those similar to them. Even as adults, we naturally gravitate towards those with a shared "nationality, ethnicity, gender, education, or career path - even the same first initial!"[13]

When it comes to a work environment, finding a level of commonality is still important, but in a different way. Rather than these surface-level similarities, it's important to look deeper - at traits that may be complementary to yours, rather than the same.

That's why when you're making choices about people, we should be using our second system of thought. When you Think Slow, you reflect, problem-solve and analyse. It's a more thorough and deliberate process that I will support you through in this chapter.[14]

How to determine the traits you're most comfortable with

Like the other areas of this book, I've not only shared *what* factors are important as you proceed with your job search (namely, finding the right people to fit in with) but I'm going to show you a proven approach to dig deep and pinpoint the traits you should look for in future co-workers and employers. These archetypal people that you feel you fit best with, make up your social core. Identifying them is the key to satisfying your need for relatedness within the workplace culture.

So, let's get down to it.

You'll start by developing a list of people you like being with. Look in social circles, family settings, work environments, clubs and teams you've been part of groups you've worked with in an education setting - they are all important.

Now, consider what attracts you to those people. You might be able to identify the traits by thinking of each person in general terms, or by thinking of specific stories that help bring this out for you.

Once you have identified the traits you are most comfortable with or are energised by, you can start to evaluate your potential work colleagues against these traits to check out their compatibility with you. Of course, for this to be successful, you should endeavour to meet as many people as you can *before you accept a position.*

Need some inspiration? Here's the story of someone who did just that:

"Three years ago Jason Guggisberg was offered the role of regional vice president at Adecco USA, the employment services company in Chicago. Before he took the job, he wanted to make sure the company was right for him. After he got the offer, he had long talks with prospective colleagues, including his potential boss, the vice president of operations, and a national sales team member.

"I asked them why they enjoyed working at Adecco, what drives them to get up in the morning, and why they had been at the company so long," he says. "Hearing their stories gave me a more well-rounded picture."[15]

An interview is an ideal time to start forming an understanding of the company culture you may be joining, as well as the job opportunity being presented to you. In fact, there are a few questions in particular that I recommend you ask in an interview to get a feel for why a job exists and whether the organisation might be a good fit for you. These are:

- Why is this role vacant?
- How long has it been vacant?
- (If it's a replacement for a previous incumbent, ask): How long was the last person in the role?
- (If less than 2 years ask): And before that?
- How would you describe the first 3 – 6 months in this role?
- What does good performance look like?
- How would you measure that performance?
- How would you describe your style of management/leadership?
- What's the team like?
- How is the team performing?

While they may seem like straightforward questions, the answers can be very telling and allow you to form a view not just of the position you're interviewing for, but the general company culture and its attitude toward employees.

You could also explain to your prospective employer that it's essential to you that you find a workplace where you fit in, and so you would appreciate meeting some other people who work there before you start. Who knows - if you do this successfully, they may be so impressed they may even make it a part of their hiring processes in future!

ACTION STEPS

1. Think of examples of people you like being with.

_____

_____

_____

_____

_____

2. Which of their attributes are you attracted to? Another way of thinking about this is: how do they enrich your day or boost your energy? Use the list of traits in Point 3 below for inspiration.

_____

_____

_____

_____

_____

3. Based on your previous answers, mark the following list of personality traits[16] you're attracted to and you should look for in future co-workers and employers.

Accessible	Courageous
Active	Courteous
Adaptable	Creative
Admirable	Cultured
Adventurous	Curious
Agreeable	Daring
Alert	Debonair
Allocentric	Decent
Amiable	Decisive
Anticipative	Dedicated
Appreciative	Deep
Articulate	Dignified
Aspiring	Directed
Athletic	Disciplined
Attractive	Discreet
Balanced	Dramatic
Benevolent	Dutiful
Brilliant	Dynamic
Calm	Earnest
Capable	Ebullient
Captivating	Educated
Caring	Efficient
Challenging	Elegant
Charismatic	Eloquent
Charming	Empathetic
Cheerful	Energetic
Clean	Enthusiastic
Clear-headed	Esthetic
Clever	Exciting
Colourful	Extraordinary
Companionly	Fair
Compassionate	Faithful
Conciliatory	Farsighted
Confident	Felicific
Conscientious	Firm
Considerate	Flexible
Constant	Focused
Contemplative	Forceful
Cooperative	Forgiving

Forthright
Freethinking
Friendly
Fun-loving
Gallant
Generous
Gentle
Genuine
Good-natured
Gracious
Hardworking
Healthy
Hearty
Helpful
Heroic
High-minded
Honest
Honourable
Humble
Humorous
Idealistic
Imaginative
Impressive
Incisive
Incorruptible
Independent
Individualistic
Innovative
Inoffensive
Insightful
Insouciant
Intelligent
Intuitive
Invulnerable
Kind
Knowledge
Leaderly
Leisurely
Liberal

Logical
Lovable
Loyal
Lyrical
Magnanimous
Many-sided
Masculine (Manly)
Mature
Methodical
Meticulous
Moderate
Modest
Multi-levelled
Neat
Non-Authoritarian
Objective
Observant
Open
Optimistic
Orderly
Organized
Original
Painstaking
Passionate
Patient
Patriotic
Peaceful
Perceptive
Perfectionist
Personable
Persuasive
Planful
Playful
Polished
Popular
Practical
Precise
Principled
Profound

WHAT'S IMPORTANT TO YOU?

Protean
Protective
Providential
Prudent
Punctual
Purposeful
Rational
Realistic
Reflective
Relaxed
Reliable
Resourceful
Respectful
Responsible
Responsive
Reverential
Romantic
Rustic
Sage
Sane
Scholarly
Scrupulous
Secure
Selfless
Self-critical
Self-defacing
Self-denying
Self-reliant
Self-sufficient
Sensitive
Sentimental
Seraphic
Serious
Sexy
Sharing
Shrewd
Simple
Skilful
Sober

Sociable
Solid
Sophisticated
Spontaneous
Sporting
Stable
Steadfast
Steady
Stoic
Strong
Studious
Suave
Subtle
Sweet
Sympathetic
Systematic
Tasteful
Teacherly
Thorough
Tidy
Tolerant
Tractable
Trusting
Uncomplaining
Understanding
Undogmatic
Unfoolable
Upright
Urbane
Venturesome
Vivacious
Warm
Well-bred
Well-read
Well-rounded
Winning
Wise
Witty
Youthful

4. What steps will you take to try to meet people before you accept a new job?

_____
_____
_____
_____
_____
_____

KEY LESSONS

Before you proceed to the next part of this book, I encourage you to revisit these lessons from the chapter you just read.

It's difficult to predict how you will feel doing a future job. But, by taking clues from your life so far, you can better anticipate the kinds of work, employers and people that will be a good fit for you.

One of these clues lies in your values. Finding a job that aligns with what you stand for will help you achieve a sense of fulfilment that is so important in life.

Next, you should strive to understand your innermost motivations. Whether you are promotion-focused (play to win) or prevention-focused (play

NOT to lose) is very telling when it comes to the particular aspects of a job or workplace culture that may appeal to you.

Who you work with is one of the most important decisions you face. Feeling comfortable with those around you is essential to satisfy one of your most innate needs - relatedness.

Relatedness is about feeling connected to those around you, and in turn, they also feel connected to you. Relatedness gives you:

- Motivation
- Enjoyment
- Better performance
- An environment of trust
- A sense of enrichment

To find that sense of relatedness, you must look to your social core and determine the traits that you're most comfortable with. Once you're aware of what these traits are, you can try to meet as many people as possible *before* you start a job and make an informed decision as to whether you and they are a good fit.

Remember! Your instinct to follow a System 1 thought system when making people decisions is

unreliable. Instead, you must think using System 2, looking deeply and thoroughly before you dive in.

In Part 3 of this book, we will explore the secrets of an enriched career and how to identify your own.

CHAPTER 7

SECRETS OF AN ENRICHED CAREER

PART 3

Your enriched career

Part 2 of this book encouraged you to self-explore, so you could uncover the building blocks of what makes you, you.

But, how do those parts of you fit with your future professional life in a way that fulfils your basic needs, as well as your higher-level ones, so that your career actually enriches your life?

In Part 3, it all comes together.

We'll begin by exploring the secrets of an enriched career so that you can avoid common career traps and pitfalls.

Then, you'll learn how to assemble the building blocks of your life so that you discover your potential, ideal career paths.

There are four common traps you may face when choosing a career:

- Believing you are only *meant* to do one thing
- That you must identify a *specific* career position to work toward
- That doing what you're *supposed* to will bring you success
- That having your base, practical needs met is enough to bring satisfaction

Let's get to the truth of these now.

The fallacy of "the one"

It's critical you embrace the idea that several paths can lead you to have a satisfying career and life. Don't get hung up on finding the "perfect" job for you. Instead, try to think of your career as always being in a state of flux.

It's dysfunctional and unrealistic to believe you only have one true calling in life, for you are capable of so much and can never predict what doors will open throughout. The pitfall of believing you can only have one purpose will lead you to being frozen with indecision trying to figure it out, or choosing something and finding it isn't as great as you'd built it up to be. In your job search, you should be looking for *ideal* paths, not the *only* one.

Stanford innovators Bill Burnett and Dave Evans, in their book *Designing Your Life*, propose an interesting way of embracing the concept of multiple potential paths. Burnett and Evans suggest sketching out three lives according to these criteria:

1. **Your Optimised Life:** You redesign your current career by reducing disengaging and exhausting tasks and increasing the tasks that engage and energise you. Do this by looking for the times you were excited, focused and having a good time at work. A perk of this approach is that when you become so good at the things you enjoy, you may be asked to do the things you don't enjoy even less, thereby maximising those enriching elements while reducing those that only deplete your energy.

2. **Your Alternate Life:** This is the life you would have if your current career vanished. In that instance, what industry would you try to transfer your skills to?

3. **Your Fascinated Life:** This life is where you see yourself doing the thing you want to do if money and image were no object. It is the dreamer's life, with no barriers to hold you back.[1]

We'll touch on this again in the next chapter when you assess your own potential career paths.

The misbelief that you can't proceed without a specific destination in mind

Rather than pinpointing the exact role you'd like to have, it's worth considering a general direction. Choosing a particular field or *type of work*, for

example, that aligns with your values, skills, achievements, interests and motivations will stand you in good stead as you start to pursue this direction.

When you think this way, rather than in terms of a specific position, you'll find this less restrictive approach allows you to be more open to opportunity. In line with this, also consider looking for work that will foster learning, so that you may grow personally and professionally, thereby continually enriching your life along the way.

The myth that success depends on doing what you're *supposed* to

Scott Dinsmore of *Live Your Legend*, advocated for forgetting about doing what you're supposed to. With 80% of the American workforce unhappy in their job, much of the problem seems to stem from people following a path they've been told to. Instead, Dinsmore said you should identify your own definition of success, because success to you doesn't have to look like everyone else's.[2]

In fact, Eric Barker, author of *Barking Up the Wrong Tree*, suggests defining success through subjective measures. According to Barker, those are:

Achievement: Do you feel like you're winning?

Legacy: Do you feel like you're influencing others in a positive way?

Significance: Do you feel like you're needed by the people closest to you?

Happiness: Do you feel like you're enjoying life?[3]

Burnett and Evans propose another way of defining what success looks like to you:

(**1**) Do you like it?

(**2**) How confident are you in it?

(**3**) Does it fit with your life, work and world-view[4]

 ACTION STEPS

Thinking about your life and career to date, answer the following questions to help you define your own measures of success:

1. What do you do now that helps you feel like you're winning?

_____

_____

_____

_____

_____

_____

2. Who do you influence positively, and how?

_____

_____

_____

_____

_____

_____

3. Who are the people closest to you that make you feel needed, and how?

_____
_____
_____
_____
_____
_____

4. Do you enjoy life, and why?

_____
_____
_____
_____
_____
_____

The trap of satisfying only basic needs

Frederick Herzberg's _Theory of Motivation_, (also known as _Two-Factor Theory or Motivation-Hygiene Theory_) tells us much about why some jobs are merely tolerable to us, and others provide the highest level of fulfilment.

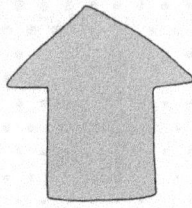

MOTIVATIONAL FACTORS

- reward
- recognition
- challenging job
- opportunity for promotion
- sense of achievement

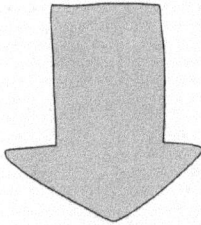

HYGIENE FACTORS

- working environment
- job security
- fringe benefits
- salary level

Herzberg proposed that it isn't just a case of being dissatisfied or satisfied with a job, but rather, that there are two sets of factors which govern negative and positive work attitudes.[5]

Hygiene factors are those governed by the context in which work is performed. They are the working environment (physical and interpersonal), the remuneration and benefits, job security and working policies. According to Herzberg, these factors relate to dissatisfaction, but they're not enough to make a career satisfying on their own. When these factors are appropriately present, they can mitigate the frustrations of a job, but don't bring high levels of performance. For that, motivating factors must also be present.

Motivating factors are intangible in the context of work, and it is these that govern whether you find a job extremely satisfying and meaningful. They are achievement, the challenge of the work itself, the recognition you receive, as well as opportunities for growth, advancement and responsibility.

This means that when looking for a meaningful career, you need to look beyond the salary or the fancy office. Those will only take you so far. When the hygiene factors are right, you then need to ask yourself if your motivators for success will be realised in your new job. Ask:

- Is it meaningful to you?
- Is it going to give you a chance to develop?
- Will you learn new things?
- Will you have the opportunity for recognition and achievement?
- Will you be given responsibility?[6]

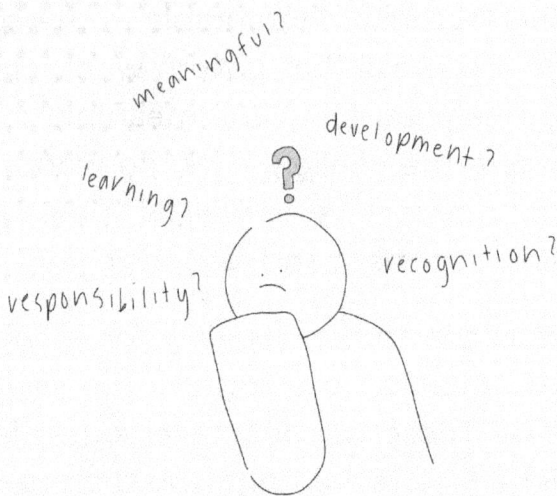

For each individual, you would expect the answers to these questions to differ, even when considering the same job. For each person's definition of success should be different. Interestingly, there are even trends across generations when it comes to what each of these things means to us.

For example, even though professional development is a motivating factor for all people, it's thought that because millennials have grown up in a world of relative peace (compared to earlier generations), they are increasingly looking for esteem and self-actualisation. And what that comes down to overall is *professional development*. They want to grow. They are seeking things out for themselves because they can. They are curious and interested in the world.

To illustrate this further, let's look at a survey-based study which compared three generations (Baby Boomers, Gen X and Millennials) and their views of work. The study identified apparent differences between the generations when asked whether the meaning of work to them was:

- A means to an end;
- Routine and life structure; or
- Challenges and opportunities.

Boomers leaned heavily towards routine and structure (77%), while Gen X and millennials favoured challenges and opportunities (47% and 56% respectively).[7]

BOOMERS

77% → routine → structure

GEN X + MILLENNIALS

47% + 56% → challenges → opportunities

Whether what motivates you fits with your generational trends or not, you need to identify what success means to you and choose a career path that fulfils this for you.

The next chapter will further explore a fulfilling career, in terms of an effective model that helps you pinpoint the enriched space at the intersection of where your strengths lie, what you love, what's important to you and what is financially viable.

If something hasn't clicked for you so far and you haven't come up with your ideal job, you don't need to be concerned. Exploring the SLIMPACT™ model will demonstrate how to bring all the different aspects together that we've examined so far - accomplishments, skills, interests, values, motivations, and the people you fit with.

Then, you can start seriously narrowing down the ideal paths you should consider following, and I'll help you understand the difference between relaunching your career into a different space, or re-dedicating yourself in the same or a related position.

KEY LESSONS

Before you proceed to the next chapter, I encourage you to revisit these lessons from the chapter you just read.

It's easy to be influenced by those around us and get hung up on set ways of doing things. Choosing a career is no exception. The trouble is, much of that influence is based on false beliefs, and, rather than see you find an enriched career, it can lead you headfirst into common career traps.

The secret to an enriched career requires you to wise up to these traps, including:

- The fallacy that there is only one thing you are meant to do
- That you must remain stagnant until you pinpoint a specific job position to move toward
- You should do what you are supposed to and live according to other's definition of success
- That only good hygiene factors, like a high salary, will be enough to satisfy you

Steering yourself away from the pitfalls and maximising the elements you *know* to enrich your life sets you on the truest course to a satisfying career.

So, when considering a job opportunity, remember to ask yourself:

- Is it meaningful to you?
- Is it going to give you a chance to develop?
- Will you learn new things?
- Will you have the opportunity for recognition and achievement?
- Will you be given responsibility?

Chapter 8 explores a way to bring all of the things you have learned so far, together. Following the SLIMPACT™ model will help you to brainstorm potential career paths.

CHAPTER 8

IDENTIFYING YOUR ENRICHED CAREER

Up to this point, you've discovered that finding a fulfilling career that enriches your life is about much more than chasing happiness, which is all too fleeting. A career should:

- Provide the opportunity for learning and development
- Give you a sense of autonomy
- Help you feel like you're winning and receive recognition for that
- Help you connect with those around you, for a sense of relatedness
- And much more

Luckily, there's a way to tie all these threads together, to help identify your enriched career.

That lies in the simple, yet powerful model, SLIMPACT™.

SLIMPACT

In this chapter, you'll learn:

- About the SLIMPACT™ model
- How to apply the SLIMPACT™ model to your own life
- How SLIMPACT™ relates to what you have learned about yourself throughout this book
- How to get a super-enriched career if you are a Purpose-driven person
- The keys to being a hopeful person when approaching a new path

ABOUT SLIMPACT™

You may have heard of the Japanese model for career choice, called Ikigai (pronounced eye-ka-guy). Ikigai aims for you to discover where your passions and talents intersect with the things that 'the world needs' and is willing to pay for.

I personally admire the Ikigai model. However I find that the majority of my coaching clients really struggle with implementing the model, especially at the point of determining what 'the world needs'.

After coaching many hundreds of people, I found a more accessible model: one which has you focussing on the intersection of **S**trengths + **L**ove + **I**mportance + **M**oney, (SLIM). It provides an easier

pathway for people to feel enriched in their career.

When some of my coaching clients go even further and add in their **P** for Purpose, it leads them to discover their own super-enriched career.

I call this approach, the SLIMPACT™ model.

When you find your SLIMPACT™ it supports you to:

- make an IMPACT when you work from your enriched spot
- make a PACT with yourself to work from your enriched spot
- ACT with Purpose and enrichment in whatever you do in your career.

Simple, yet powerful, I have seen people transform their careers using the SLIMPACT™ model. It can also do the same for you.

Working on your SLIMPACT™ is the most critical lesson contained within this book for finding a career that contributes to an overall enriched and fulfilled life.

BRINGING IT TOGETHER

In Part 2 of this book, I explained that the building blocks making up your life are the key to finding your enriched career. Now you've identified *your* building blocks, it's time to understand what they mean in the context of choosing your next career.

Your strengths are, simply put, what you are good at.

In Chapter 4, we referred to these as your *skills* (functional, formal and personality skills) and *accomplishments*. They may encompass what you are naturally good at, but also what you have worked hard to achieve over time. In other words, they are your competencies, which, according to *Self-Determination Theory*, are one of three things vital to a fulfilling career.[1]

A career that harnesses your strengths not only ensures you achieve higher levels of performance, but it also builds confidence and leads to higher levels of job satisfaction as you flourish in your role.

What you love is an easy piece of the career puzzle to figure out. This component encompasses all those things that seem to enrich your life innately. These are the things you are drawn to, where you

seem to lose time because you enjoy what you're doing so completely.

In Chapter 5, we referred to these as your *interests*. What is also important to remember is that interests come in several forms, namely: people interests, informational interests, and object interests.

A career that incorporates what you love keeps you committed and engaged with what you do, and is, therefore, an essential component of a successful career.

What's important to you represents what you stand for and the culture you are drawn to.

In Chapter 6, we referred to these as your values, motivations and your social core.

It's crucial you are clear about what you do and don't stand for, in terms of the values you hold, the values the organisation holds, what motivates you, and the traits of the people you best fit with. When you are clear on these, you'll be more discerning about the type of work you want to do and the workplace culture you want to be part of.

In other words, you'll be equipped to identify a workplace that you fit with, because it employs people with personality traits you gel with, and also

shares the values that have meaning to you.

When you feel as though you fit with the workplace culture, you'll have a sense of affinity with your employer and team members, fostering that all-important sense of relatedness that *Self-Determination Theory* says is critical to an enriched career.[2]

What you can get paid for is not about finding the highest-paying job. You've already learned that money is one of Herzberg's hygiene factors and that while not having enough of it can breed dissatisfaction, the more you are paid doesn't determine that you'll find a career fulfilling.

Instead, the money component refers to finding a financially-viable career. After all, one reason we work is to support our lifestyles and families, so you need to choose a job that will be able to provide for those things.

For an enriched career, you need all four of these components to be satisfied. A career with one of these missing will only deplete you.

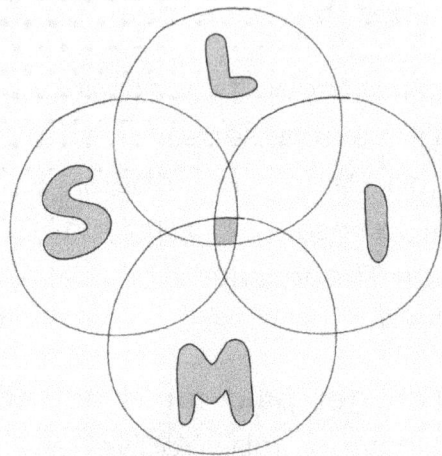

The following action steps are designed to help you assess if your current or recent position is fulfilling, according to the SLIMPACT™ model and the self-assessment you have done in the previous chapters.

If you are a recent graduate and don't have an existing job to analyse, you may skip this set of action steps and move to the next section entitled: *Action steps (including new graduates).*

ACTION STEPS

IF YOU ARE CURRENTLY EMPLOYED/RECENTLY LEFT A JOB

Below, you will see four buckets correlating to the four components of the SLIMPACT™ model. Each also relates to answers you provided in previous chapters, so make sure you have these on hand.

Now, think about your current job, or one from your past, and mark each bucket according to how the position "fills these up" for you.

STRENGTHS	LOVE	IMPORTANCE	MONEY
→ consider the skills and achievements you listed in ch. 4	→ consider the interests you listed in ch 5	→ consider the values, motivations and personality traits you listed in ch. 6	→ is it financially viable? → are your hygiene factors fulfilled? ch. 7

Now, write about how satisfied you are with those levels. Do not skip this step - this is very revealing.

1. Strengths

_____
_____
_____
_____
_____
_____

2. Love

_____
_____
_____
_____
_____
_____

3. Importance

_____
_____
_____
_____
_____
_____

4. Money

_____
_____
_____
_____
_____
_____

Your results

There's no magic number to say whether your buckets are full enough to stick with your job - only you can decide that. But a visual representation can make things glaringly obvious to you.

What did you find? Were you happy with the majority of the buckets, but found one is lacking? There might be a way to redesign your job, rather than have a complete change of paths. We'll talk about the idea of re-dedicating to your current path in the next chapter.

If you are clearly dissatisfied, not sure, or want to explore your options (good choice) then move to the next action step to look at alternative career paths for you.

ACTION STEPS

(INCLUDING NEW GRADUATES)

Everyone, including new graduates, should answer the following questions in order to identify their enriched career, which exists at the intersection of **S**trengths + **L**ove + **I**mportance + **M**oney.

1. What are you good at?

Drawing on the skills and accomplishments you identified in Chapter 4, write 5-8 lines on these and how they could show up in a career.

_____
_____
_____
_____
_____

2. What do you love?

Drawing on the interests you identified in Chapter 5, write 5-8 lines on these and how they could show up in a career.

_____
_____
_____
_____
_____

3. What's important to you?

Drawing on the values, motivations and personality traits you identified in Chapter 6, write 5-8 lines on how these could show up in a career and your idea of an ideal company culture.

_____

_____

_____

_____

_____

4. What can you get paid for?

Using your answers from the three previous questions, what potential career paths (that you can get paid for) can you think of? Write them all down, no matter how far fetched they may seem.

_____

_____

_____

_____

_____

5. Now, you're going to rank your potential paths according to the criteria we discussed in Chapter 7. Fill out the following table - ranking each path on a) how much you like it, b) how confident you are in it and c) whether it fits with your life view, work view, and world view.[3]
(score from 1 to 5, with 5 being the highest)

6. Total the scores you awarded each one to reveal your top ranking career paths.

Potential job	A How much you like it *(score 1 to 5)*	B How confident you are in it *(score 1 to 5)*	C Whether it fits with your life view, work view, and world view *(score 1 to 5)*	Total score

7. What are your top five jobs? Do these fall into any of the three designed life paths I introduced you to in chapter 7? Project your life and imagine how your potential careers paths will fit.[4]

- Your Optimised Life (your current career, redesigned)

_____

_____

_____

_____

_____

- Your Alternate Life (the one you would transfer your existing skills too)

_____

_____

_____

_____

_____

- Your Fascinated Life (what you would want to do if there were no barriers)

_____

_____

_____

_____

_____

WHAT ABOUT PURPOSE?

For many people, finding the intersection of their **S**trengths + **L**ove + **I**mportance + **M**oney (SLIM) in a job is enough to enrich their lives. They go on to enjoy a fulfilling career that satisfies them in a way they never believed possible.

However, others may like to go deeper and also ensure their potential career includes a sense of Purpose, to achieve what I call a super-enriched career.

Caveat: considering Purpose in your career is an optional step. You can absolutely enjoy a fulfilling career path without identifying your Purpose. However, if you feel as though you are a *Purpose-driven* person, then I'd encourage you to consider this additional component to the career model.

The additional 'Purpose' component is the **P** of the SLIMPACT™ model. It super-enriches your career, allowing you to really hone in on the way in which you will make an IMPACT thereby living with Purpose.

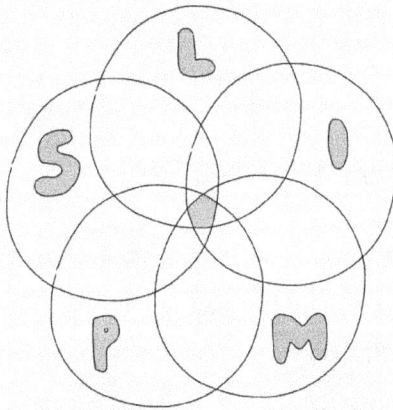

If you are *Purpose-driven*, you desire to create an impact bigger than yourself, and so this more complex model asks you to identify *why* you do what you do.

Your *why* does not merely come from your head. It is not cerebral. It must be from your mind, body and core.

In his best-selling book, *Start with Why*, Simon Sinek related that only when he learned to articulate why he did what he did, did his life start to turn around. He stopped talking about *what* he did and only started talking about what he *believed*.[5]

He said that people who believed what he believed in, wanted to learn more. He was magnetic.

Here are two examples of a magnetic *why* that I workshopped with my coaching clients:

1. "My Dad died when I was 10. He did not need to die. But in those days, he was unable to receive quality health care. From the day he died, having seen what tragically happened to him and the impact his passing had on the rest of my family, I decided to dedicate my life to making sure that people – no matter what their background, their demographic or circumstances – would receive better health services."

(2) "In the space of one year, I attended 70 funerals of family and community members – most of whom were aged between 37 and 52 in remote parts of my home state. I was so overcome by the injustice and the inequality of services and support to people in remote areas, that I quit my successful career as a plumber and made a commitment that people in remote areas would never endure such suffering ever again."

Now it's time for you to write yours.

ACTION STEPS

In crafting your magnetic why, I want you to answer these questions:

1. What triggered you to start on your own journey?

_____
_____
_____
_____
_____
_____

2. What stories along the way helped to reinforce that your journey was on the right path for you?

_____
_____
_____
_____
_____
_____

3. What do you believe in?

_____
_____
_____
_____
_____
_____

4. What have you dedicated your life to?

_____
_____
_____
_____
_____
_____

5. What are you committed to?

_____
_____
_____
_____
_____
_____

6. Why do you get out of bed in the morning, and why should anyone care?

_____
_____
_____
_____
_____
_____

7. What is the visceral, core reason you do what you do?

_____
_____
_____
_____
_____
_____

If you can identify your magnetic why, it's often easy to see that it relates to something that the world needs from you. You can see from the examples above that the world does indeed need:

(1) Quality health services

(2) Support services in remote areas

ACTION STEPS

1. What does the world need that you would like to, or can provide? Consider your why.

_____

_____

_____

_____

_____

2. How does this tie in with, what your strengths are, what you love, what's important to you and what you can get paid for, to identify a potential career?

_____

_____

_____

_____

_____

THE NEED FOR HOPE

As you complete the action steps in this chapter and look toward the paths in front of you, I ask one thing: that you remain hopeful.

According to Shane J. Lopez, author of *Making Hope Happen*, hopeful people believe these two things:

- "There are many paths to my goals
- None of them are free of obstacles"[6]

Similarly, Robert Greene, author of *Mastery*, suggests the importance of patience and attention to detail. You should not be in a hurry to make a splash with your career. That means watching for the false path (like careers you might be attracted to for the wrong reasons) and learning to rebel against any forces pushing you from your true path.[7]

When approaching a career transition or even re-dedicating yourself to the path you are currently on, having this resourceful attitude will help you maintain momentum, be resilient and create staying power on your road to success.

KEY LESSONS

Before you proceed to the next chapter, I encourage you to revisit these lessons from the chapter you just read.

SLIMPACT

The SLIMPACT™ model is a simple, yet highly-effective framework for choosing a career that enriches your life. Looking at a culmination of your skills and achievements, your interests, what is important to you and what is financially-viable helps you identify pathways that are highly-engaging and bring out the best in you, in terms of staying committed and performing well.

When you don't satisfy all four of these components together, there will be a nagging sense of dissatisfaction that ultimately depletes your life, rather than enriching it.

If you are a Purpose-driven person, then you will benefit from applying the P in the SLIMPACT™

model, which includes the optional component *Purpose*. Identifying your *why* will help you pinpoint your potential pathways for a super-enriched career.

As you hone in on your career options and get closer to identifying your future, fulfilling career, remember to stay hopeful and resilient.

Chapter 9 brings an opportunity for you to think further on the choice to re-dedicate or re-launch before you make any decisions.

CHAPTER 9

BECOME EMPLOYABLE LONG-TERM

PART 3

Your enriched career

Choosing a set career path based on your preferences is one thing. And right now, you might be able to imagine doing it for 20 years. But what happens if you change your mind, an industry is influenced to change their approach or technology renders your position obsolete?

There is no way to predict what will happen in the future and I'm not suggesting you try to do so. But I am suggesting you think about a career in terms of its potential to help you with long-term employability, rather than long-term employment.

LONG TERM EMPLOYABILITY > LONG TERM EMPLOYMENT

When you consider a particular position or a potential career path, think if it will help you adapt your transferable skills, encourage your determination to adapt to changes around you and give you the opportunity to create added value.

This chapter will help you understand a contemporary and forward-looking view of a valuable employee, and the benefits of reapplying

yourself to your current path vs. launching your career anew. By the end of this chapter, you should be able to visualise the best direction to take as you move towards a fulfilling career.

PERFORMANCE IS OVERRATED

Claudio Fernandez-Araoz, author of *It's Not the How or the What But the Who*, writes that talent selection in the 1980s focused heavily on performance as an indicator of who is right for a role. In fact, he says the mantra was "the best predictor of future success is past success."[1] You might have been led to believe something similar.

But today, other factors are equally, if not more important as predictors of success in the workplace. These factors are not just what will get you hired now, but help you have a sustainable career, where you adapt for longevity in employability, rather than a long-held position.

According to Monique Valcour, "a sustainable career is dynamic and flexible; it features continuous learning, periodic renewal, the security that comes from employability, and a harmonious fit with your skills, interests, and values."[2] It's a career focused on continued growth rather than just checking the boxes.

This is why, for many industries, there are now multiple pathways for entry. In careers where the supply of tertiary-qualified people isn't meeting demand, entry requirements are being relaxed, periods of training shortened or delivered in different modes and more individual approaches welcomed.

Let's talk about this in the context of an institutional vs. vocational approach. For example, consider a person who has led a purely academic life, compared to someone who has practical life experience.

The person with practical experience has likely had more of an opportunity to develop and demonstrate their potential. They have formed skills and achievements within the workplace and have

learned to add value to a company while on the job.

Academic life certainly has its place, but you can see how long-term employability depends on more intangible factors than looking good on paper. Let's explore some of those factors now.

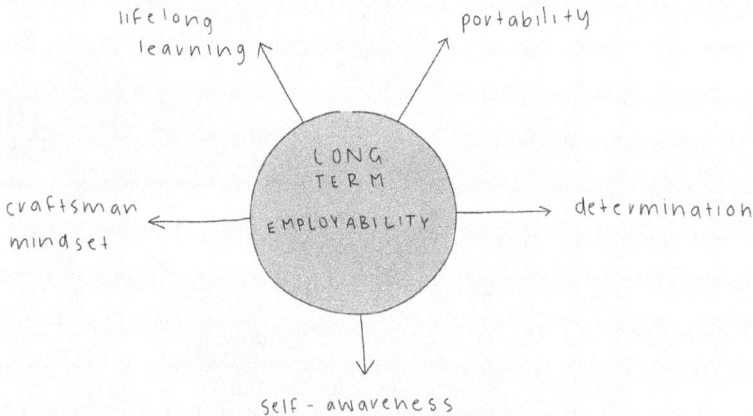

lifelong learning

portability

LONG TERM EMPLOYABILITY

craftsman mindset

determination

self - awareness

PORTABILITY

According to Fernandez-Araoz, "the best employees and executives are what talent management experts call portable. They are able to effectively transition from one role, company, industry, or country to the next, not only bringing their unique strengths to each but also growing stronger in the process."[3]

Technology is changing so rapidly that predicting

what specific skills will matter most to employers in even two years is impossible. That's why traits like flexibility, dynamism and growth in non-linear careers are so highly valued.

Interestingly, a Foundation for Young Australians (FYA) report published in 2016, entitled *The New Work Mindset*, found that particular skills can be more portable than expected. Analysis of more than 2.7 million job advertisements revealed that working in one job helps a person develop skills for 13 other positions.[4]

According to FYA CEO, Jan Owen, "this report shows our mindset needs to shift to reflect a more dynamic future of work where linear careers are less likely to exist and young people will need a portfolio of skills and capabilities, including career management skills, to navigate multiple roles within a jobs cluster."[5]

In fact, the report proposes a new strategy should be implemented, to focus (in part) on providing young people with "the skills to craft and navigate multiple careers."[6] This clearly demonstrates that the "one career" mindset is flawed, and we need to make room collectively and individually for the notion of long-term employability.

DETERMINATION

Another trait key to long-term employability is determination. Embracing the need to grow throughout your working life, rather than looking for somewhere you can just "settle in" will see you remain flexible and more prepared for any future professional disruption or transition. I'm not advocating for the death of your commitment to a role or an employer, but it's essential your expectations are in line with reality.

Employers appreciate people determined to push past obstacles and who have a strong motivation to be the best they can be.[7] You can do this too, by becoming increasingly valuable, updating your skillset and embracing new technologies, processes and working environments.

SELF-AWARENESS

When you know yourself well, you're equipped to identify places of interest to you, and where you can be confident of adding value. This means instead of just fulfilling duties, you'll bring something new and vital to the workplace culture, processes, brand and customer service attitudes, for example.

Knowing yourself means understanding where your

strengths and weaknesses lie, and what energises you.[8] That's why this is the focus of Part 2 of this book. You learned to not only better understand your next career move, but are also more prepared for those that may follow it.

CRAFTSMAN MINDSET

According to Newport, when you're focused on discovering and pursuing your "passion", you're projecting a view of "what can the world offer me?"[9] While this may sound good in terms of achieving personal fulfilment, it is a problematic mindset for having career longevity and long-term employability.

If passion does show up for you, you'll find that it ebbs and flows like the tide. When your career depends on passion, you become fixed in your mentality, open to less flexibility and seemingly, unreliable.

On the other hand, a *craftsman mindset* asks "what can I offer the world?" You have a determined focus on constantly improving at your craft and as a result, become uniquely valuable to the team, company and your customers. When you adopt a *craftsman mindset* in your job search, the best question you can ask yourself is: "will I love the process of getting better at this?"[10]

BEING A LIFELONG LEARNER

In addition to having a craftsman mindset, being willing to commit to lifelong learning is essential if you want to remain at the top of your chosen profession.

According to a report by McKinsey & Company, between September 2009 and June 2012, there's been a significant increase in the number of skill sets needed in the workforce: up from 178 to 924.[11]

No matter how you were trained as a school-leaver, it's clear that this education will not be enough to keep you skilled and employable long-term.

But, when you're committed to the concept of lifelong learning, it changes everything. *Lifelong learning* is the ongoing, voluntary and self-motivated pursuit of knowledge for either personal or professional reasons.

According to Robert Greene, author of *Mastery*, "the future belongs to those who learn more skills and combine them in creative ways." This is because those who are trained to handle complexities, to organise information well, and intersect knowledge from various fields are more valuable than those overwhelmed and distracted from learning.[12]

Lifelong learning also brings with it a sense of excitement as you realise that just because your formal education years are behind you, you will still get to experience the challenge and accomplishment that comes from expanding your skills and knowledge base.

While it helps you stay at the top of your game, you are no longer tied to a particular industry or role for the rest of your days - there is plenty of room for growth and new beginnings too. You can discover new interests, newfound confidence in your abilities and meet entirely different networks of people you may never have crossed paths with before.

So, how do you practise lifelong learning? Here's one strategy I recommend for rapid learning of a new skill.

LEARN FAST

In his book *The First 20 Hours*, Josh Kaufman[13] helps people understand that if you follow the right process, you can become proficient at any new skill in just under 20 hours, or 40 minutes every day for a month.

According to Kaufman, accelerated learning, or "rapid skill acquisition" does not require memorising the minutiae and it's important to approach it differently to academic learning. Instead, you should aim to immerse yourself in the central aspects so you can add that skill to your skillset permanently.

To put it in perspective, think for a moment about learned skills that you've been able to transfer (at least in part) from one job to another. This is entirely different from the 'cramming' you did at school to just pass your exams - only to promptly forget most of what you'd learned.

According to Kaufman,[14] these five steps will help you learn anything quickly.

(1) Define what you want to learn

This includes your preferred "target performance level". Be specific and keep fine-tuning your goal until you know precisely what you want to learn and what that involves.

(2) Break down the skill into its basic components

Most skills are not merely single skills. Instead, they are made up of a collection of sub-skills. Taking the example of golf. Driving and putting are stand-alone skills with little in common, but both are essential to the game. Kaufman suggests fragmenting your goal into its most rudimentary parts, then focus on practising the most crucial sub-skills.

(3) **Identify the critical sub-skills involved in reaching your goal**

Review 3-5 helpful resources such as manuals, videos or online tutorials. Browse them to identify the tips that are common to all resources. Build an understanding of how to improve in those areas. Practise those sub-skills first and repeat as often as you can.

(4) **Eliminate any obstacles to practising**

Eliminate all distractions so you can conduct focused, uninterrupted practice in peace. Make it easy to find and use the equipment, so you have nil justification for not practising.

(5) **Commit to at least 20 hours of deliberate focused practice**

Don't be concerned if at first you are low on the learning curve and perform poorly. Put in a reasonable time commitment that will support your continuing rather than quitting.

There is research that suggests people advance fastest in the beginning when they lack skill. As you deliberately practise, you will progress through three stages of learning:

- You will consciously think about every tiny detail of the skill

- Some skills will come to you more naturally with less effort

- Eventually, with repetition, new skills become instinctive

  Your first 20 hours of practice will get you to a solid level of performance.

It's important to note: I don't just advocate lifelong learning for where it can take your career, but the significant impact it can have on your personal development too.

Now that you understand the makings of long-term employability for your career, how will you decide whether you need a fresh approach or to re-dedicate yourself to your current one?

TO RE-DEDICATE OR RE-LAUNCH?

Have you reached a fork in the road and can't decide which option to take? You might be:

- A recent graduate, unsure if you still want to do what you set out to
- A recent graduate who has realised their degree opens unexpected doors into alternative pathways
- An employee moving on from redundancy
- Someone who has held a variety of jobs, but never found where they fit
- A highly experienced and long-term employee considering a significant change
- Re-evaluating whether your life would be more fulfilled by pursuing a different path

If this is you, you could benefit from a deep-dive into the exploration of the two different career strategies: re-dedicating and re-launching.

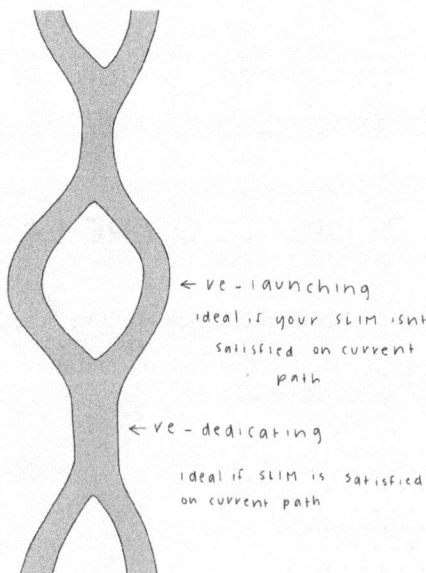

← re-launching
ideal if your SLIM isnt
satisfied on current
path

← re-dedicating
ideal if SLIM is satisfied
on current path

Re-dedicating

Re-dedicating is ideal if the analysis of your current situation reveals it satisfies hygiene factors for you, and also maximises motivating factors. It won't be perfect - no job is. There are always daily frustrations or things you would prefer not to do. But can you manage these with a combination of a mindset adjustment, re-negotiating aspects of your role with your employer, or even looking for the same position, but in a company that is a better fit for your values?

Re-dedicating may also be a good option for you if your current role requires you to wear many hats. Have you considered finding a job that requires you to utilise more of just one of these hats? This opens up your options considerably without starting entirely anew.

A sideways move can be a great way to make the changes you need, without a complete overhaul. And remember, when you're re-dedicating you want to look for ways to enhance those motivating factors, like opportunities for growth, work that provides a challenge and gives you responsibility.

ACTION STEPS

1. How could you re-dedicate yourself to your current position/career path?

_____
_____
_____
_____
_____

2. Would it satisfy your hygiene **and** motivating factors? Why/why not?

_____
_____
_____
_____
_____

Re-launching

Re-launching is ideal if (through completing the exercises in this book and careful analysis) you have realised your current or most recent job is unfulfilling in several aspects. Perhaps you've gained clarity and can point to particular factors of why it isn't a good fit for you, and how it isn't satisfying the SLIMPACT™ model.

This might even come as a relief because it provides some guidance for what to seek out from here. For instance, you may have realised you love the industry but the type of work doesn't allow for development. Or, there is a small part of the job you find intensely satisfying, so you decide to explore other positions where this plays a more dominant role.

ACTION STEPS

1. How could you re-launch your career?

_____
_____
_____
_____
_____
_____

2. Is this a better way to satisfy your hygiene **and** motivating factors? Why/why not?

_____
_____
_____
_____
_____
_____

It isn't clear cut, but following the action steps in this book and looking at your options through a lens of self-awareness will make it easier.

And don't worry. I'm not leaving you here. For there are some simple but highly-effective strategies to test out the options you're considering before you commit. But first, there's something else I want to draw your attention to: just how well-planned out should your career be?

A cycle of deliberate and emergent approaches

Clayton Christensen suggests two approaches to a career should play a role at different times in your life. Those are deliberate and emergent strategies.

If you're reading this book, I would say there's a good chance you're looking for a deliberate strategy to pursue. When it comes to your future career, you want to know what the right answer is and what to do about it. But it's not always that simple - and that's a good thing. A deliberate strategy is ideal if you are clear on which outlet satisfies your hygiene and motivating factors, and can safely pursue it.[15]

2 approaches to a career

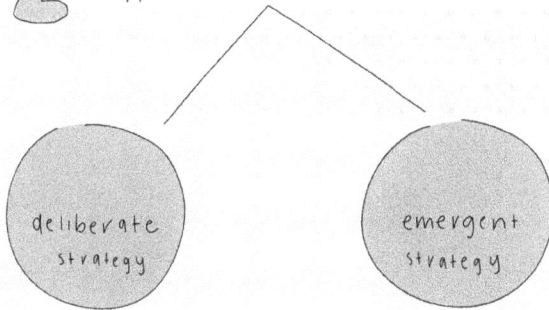

deliberate strategy

emergent strategy

If this isn't you, you will be like many of us who need to use an emergent strategy. That means making informed decisions about your career, under the guise of an experiment. If it doesn't go entirely to plan, you pivot - either by taking an opportunity presented to you or finding ways to build in more of your motivating factors. An emergent strategy can be exciting, helping you discover new pathways for your life that you'd never anticipated - and learning much about yourself in the process.[16]

Remember too that even if you have a deliberate strategy and it works for a time, you will likely go through cycles of deliberate and emergent strategies throughout your life. So don't get too hung up on finding that perfect deliberate strategy right now.

ACTION STEPS

1. Do you see a deliberate strategy working for you right now? Why/why not?

_____

_____

_____

_____

_____

2. Do you see an emergent strategy working for you right now? Why/why not?

_____

_____

_____

_____

_____

KEY LESSONS

Before you proceed to the next chapter, I encourage you to revisit these lessons from the chapter you just read.

Performance used to be the only thing that mattered to employers - and they hired accordingly. But with the changing face of the working world, new ways

of measuring potential hires have become just as important, if not more important.

What this means is, rather than looking for a job under the guise of remaining in it long-term, you need to focus on your long-term employability. To be an attractive candidate now, and in the future, you need these qualities:

- Portability
- Determination
- Self-awareness
- A craftsman mindset
- Commitment to lifelong learning

When you are dynamic and flexible in your approach to work and understand that careers today are more likely to be non-linear in nature, you're an attractive candidate. And you're also setting your working life up for success in the long-term.

But, how do you know whether to completely overhaul your career or reapply yourself to your current path?

Rededicating yourself is ideal if you have found through reading this book that your current career path fills your buckets, satisfies hygiene factors and maximises motivating factors. It may need some

adjustments, but you can see how these can be achieved.

Relaunching should be explored if your current path is unfulfilling, satisfying the criteria of the SLIMPACT™ model seems far out of reach, or you've realised there is a pathway that can better meet your needs and motivations.

Remember - every career requires an approach that varies from deliberate planning to an emergent strategy throughout your life. The trick is knowing which is the right one for you to embrace now.

Part 4 brings you to the concluding chapters of this book, preparing you to take action by testing your career options and learning how to convey who you are in the opportune moments.

CHAPTER 10

TEST THE WATERS

PART 4

Preparing for Action

Deciding which career path to pursue can be difficult.

It's difficult to stay true to your motivations, without succumbing to your natural weaknesses (as is the case with promotion vs. prevention thinking).

It's difficult not to second-guess yourself.

It's difficult to conceive of putting your time and energy into something that may not work out as expected.

But what you can do is implement some effective testing techniques, so you move forward with your decision confidently and with your eyes open.

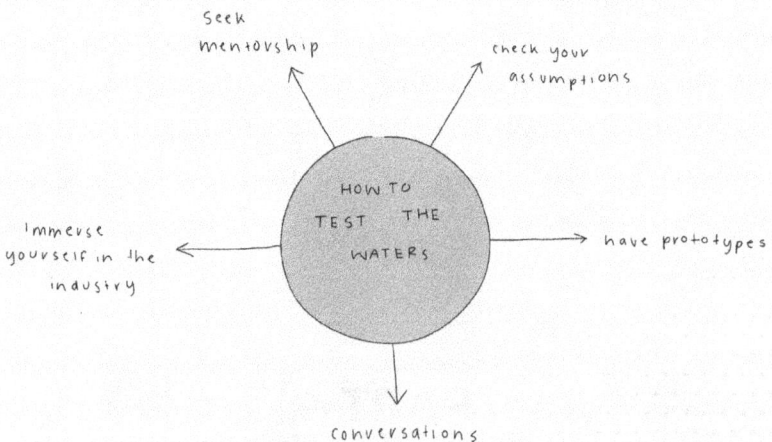

Seek
mentorship

check your
assumptions

HOW TO
TEST THE
WATERS

Immerse
yourself in the
industry

have prototypes

conversations

In this chapter you'll learn:

- How to check your assumptions about a career or specific position
- How to have Prototype Conversations
- How to immerse yourself in the industry to see if it holds your interest
- Why you should seek mentorship
- Tips for making your decision

CHECK YOUR ASSUMPTIONS

In *How Will You Measure Your Life*, Clayton Christensen asks "what has to prove true for this to work?" When you make a decision as important as what type of work you will do, and imagine yourself in the role, you inherently form assumptions about how it will go. Those beliefs might relate to many things, including:

- How your co-workers will receive you
- What needs to be delivered by others for you to succeed
- What opportunities will be presented to you for you to feel satisfied

It's so easy to form assumptions, but having them fulfilled is another matter entirely. Christensen suggests checking your assumptions by looking at them through a lens of: "are these within your control."[1] Of course, it's easier for assumptions to prove true when they only depend on you. But when part of them depend on others, it is harder to foresee the result.

Another lens for checking your assumptions is "what evidence do you have?"[2] Evidence might be related to what a potential employer promises you or how you feel about something.

If you have felt a certain way about a situation or task in the past, that is evidence you will likely continue to feel that way in the future. For example, if you have always found daily interaction with customers enriching, that is evidence you will probably feel the same way in your new role.

As for finding evidence about things outside of your control, like assumptions based on the impressions a potential employer has given you, the next step will help you assess these too - having Prototype Conversations.

ACTION STEPS

1. List your assumptions about each potential career path.

_____

_____

_____

_____

_____

2. How can you test them? Look at each assumption individually, through the lenses:
- are these within your control

and
- what evidence do you have?

_____

_____

_____

_____

_____

PROTOTYPE CONVERSATIONS

Sometimes the best way to find out if what you believe to be true about a job or industry, is actually true, is to talk to someone already living the life you want. Burnett and Evans call these Prototype Conversations or Life Design Interviews.[3]

223

What are they exactly? Well, you ask the person with experience in that area, or already doing what you're contemplating, to sit down over a coffee and share their story.

This is not set up to be an "in" to the industry or to find out if they can get you a job. *It's not about you at all.* "The story you're after is the personal story of how that person got to be doing that thing he or she does, or got the expertise he has and what it's really like to do what she does."[4]

It's an opportunity to find out what they do and don't like about the position, what surprised them about it when they started, and how they actually found themselves getting there. That means that your part in the conversation is to ask questions, not to talk about yourself. It's like an interview in this way, but your only stake in the discussion is to gather as much useful information as possible.

I'm a huge believer in when you need more information, you sit down with someone directly and find it out. No amount of Google searches or emails will substitute for a Prototype Conversation.

By the way, don't stop at one - after all, everyone's experience is different, and you want a full picture of your potential job before diving in. Try to have as many Prototype Conversations as possible.

However, you can certainly supplement your Prototype Conversations with some general industry knowledge - more on this next.

ACTION STEPS

1. Talk to your existing network to see if they can refer you to someone who is suitable for a Prototype Conversation. If you can't identify any connections that way, try searching Linkedin. List those connections here:

_____

_____

_____

_____

After you have your Prototype Conversations, answer these questions for each person you spoke to:

2. What made the biggest impact on you from your conversation?

_____

_____

_____

_____

_____

3. Did what they like or dislike about the job surprise you? Did it impact how you feel about pursuing the job?

_____

_____

_____

_____

_____

_____

4. What did you learn about their pathway into that position that could be helpful to you?

_____

_____

_____

_____

_____

_____

5. Are you as confident as you were before the conversation about pursuing this path? More confident/less confident - why?

_____

_____

_____

_____

_____

_____

6. Do you still feel as though this path will enrich your life? Or has that changed and you are concerned it may deplete it?

_____

_____

_____

_____

_____

_____

7. Is this still a path you are going to pursue?

_____

_____

_____

_____

_____

_____

INDUSTRY IMMERSION

When you love what you do for work, it's natural to become immersed in the industry - and to want to do so. Instead of waiting until you start work to see if this happens for you, why not jump right in and see if being immersed in the industry excites you now?

Alexandra Cavoulacos and Kathryn Minshew,

authors of *The New Rules of Work*, suggest learning more about the industry you're considering joining by turning to:

- Industry blogs
- Newsletters
- Conferences
- Events
- Podcasts[5]

If there are a few key players you're hoping to find employment with, look for company-specific publications about them and start following industry leaders on social media to learn about the issues that have their attention right now.

If you do all this before you actively pursue a position you'll enjoy these benefits:

- You'll identify holes in your knowledge about an industry
- You might be able to identify specific areas or issues that you already know how to add value to, or can make a focus of your learning
- You'll perform better in the job application and interview process
- But perhaps most importantly right now, you'll get a better feel if this is a wise path for you to pursue

ACTION STEPS

1. In what ways are you going to immerse yourself in the industry?

_____
_____
_____
_____
_____

After you have done so, answer these questions:

2. What have you discovered that made the biggest impact on you?

_____
_____
_____
_____
_____

3. What holes in your knowledge have you uncovered/where do you need to direct your focus further?

_____
_____
_____
_____
_____

4. Has what you learned impacted how you feel about pursuing an opportunity in this industry?

_____

_____

_____

_____

_____

_____

5. Are you as confident as you were beforehand about pursuing this path? More confident/less confident - why?

_____

_____

_____

_____

_____

_____

6. Do you still feel as though this path will enrich your life? Or has that changed and you are concerned it may deplete it?

_____

_____

_____

_____

_____

_____

7. Is this still a path you are going to pursue?

_____

_____

_____

_____

_____

_____

SEEK MENTORSHIP

To take Prototype Conversations to the next level you need to seek mentorship. I do not suggest you enter into each Prototype Conversation for the purpose of finding out if they would be a suitable (and willing) mentor, but it can be a convenient progression in the right circumstances.

Transitions are a particularly good time to seek out a mentor because it's helpful to get first-hand advice from someone who has walked the path you are on right now.

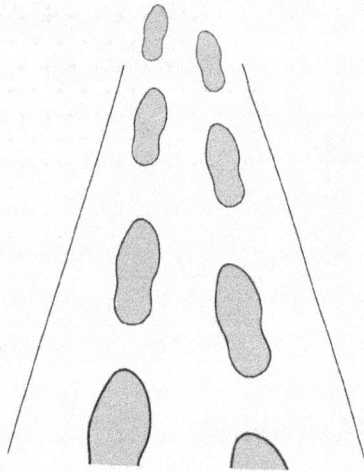

According to Greene, a mentor can offer "support, confidence, direction, space to discover things on your own." They can "gauge the extent of our progress, the weaknesses in our character, the ordeals we must go through to advance."[6]

If you're hesitant to pursue a new career path on your own or want to give yourself the best chance of succeeding, a mentor can be very helpful.

There are a number of myths associated with mentorship. Amy Gallo, a contributing editor at Harvard Business Review, points out several that are worth taking note of when considering mentorship.[7]

(1) You need one perfect mentor

You may be lucky enough to have the opportunity to turn to several people for advice. If you do, you should take advantage of that. There is no reason to limit yourself to just one person. If anything, having a small network of mentors will give you a more well-rounded level of support as you work out if you are on the right path.

(2) You (and they) need to be in it for the long-haul

You may be wondering whether it's fair to seek mentorship if you're just testing the waters of a potential career path. But, in today's fast-paced world, a long-term relationship can be unrealistic and a difficult time demand. Don't go into mentorship seeking a commitment from your mentor. Simply seek them out at the times you'd like their advice and let the relationship build from there.

(3) It's all about you

It can be difficult to ask someone to spare their time if there's nothing in it for them and you certainly shouldn't expect that from them. Instead, look for ways you can provide them with value too, so it's not just a one-sided exchange. According to Gallo, "even the promise of future help ... can be enough to convince a mentor to give up his or her time and energy."[8]

THE PSYCHOLOGY OF CHOICE

Some people find decision-making easier than others, and anxiety often accompanies making "life" decisions, like what to do for work. Luckily, there are a few tips that can help you move forward, instead of being frozen with indecision.

① Use your gut to make the final call

You've worked hard throughout this book, delving deep into your values and interests, your past experience and how you are motivated. You've weighed options against each other and considered the benefits of different paths.

But if you're having trouble choosing between your final couple of options, it's helpful to consider that intuitively, deep-down, you know what you should do. Don't discredit your gut. When you "test" a path, you innately know what feels right and what doesn't. Go with it.

② Think of regret

Although I usually advocate for focusing on the positive, if you can see yourself as being happy with each of two options, sometimes considering regret is the right approach. Which of the two options, if you didn't choose them, would leave you regretting that one of your highest values wasn't being fulfilled?

③ Know that "this isn't the final decision"

Take the anxiety away and trust that whatever you decide to do right now about your career, won't be for life. After all, that's the very nature of the world, technology and life itself - ever-changing, with new opportunities presenting themselves along the way.[9]

KEY LESSONS

Before you proceed to the next chapter, I encourage you to revisit these lessons from the chapter you just read.

Unless this is a time-sensitive issue for you, I'd suggest that you don't need to jump headfirst into a new career.

There are several avenues you can take to confirm that this will be a good move for you.

The first is to check your assumption. Assumptions that are outside your control can distort the reality of a particular career path or position.

Taking the time to assess those that are outside your control and also weighing up the evidence will help you see more clearly and be more prepared for the reality of what awaits.

Secondly, line up several Prototype Conversations. Talking to people who have found themselves in the same position you're interested in can help you weigh up if it's what you expected and whether you still want to pursue it.

Thirdly, immerse yourself in the industry. Exposing yourself to as much industry-specific information as possible before you actively seek out a position will help you decide if it excites you as much as you anticipated and that it feels right.

Finally, seeking mentorship will not only help you decide if you want to continue down a pathway but also support you as you navigate any challenges.

Chapter 11 helps you develop ways to articulate who you are and what your path is before you start pursuing work.

CHAPTER 11

CONVEY WHO YOU ARE

PART 4

Preparing for Action

"Tell me about yourself."

I can guarantee every person has been asked this question. Whether on an awkward first date, in a networking environment or of course, in a job interview.

The funny thing is, that when people ask this vague and mundane question, what they really want is to be wowed in response.

Unfortunately, that's what they rarely get.

Like most people, when you answer with the default - a regurgitation of basic facts or milestones from your life, they are hardly intrigued enough to want to continue the conversation. In fact, I'll bet you've witnessed that glazed-eyed look as they wait for you to stop talking so they can move onto someone else.

But, what if you met this question with enthusiasm and a storied approach? Instead, you could take this connection into new territory and propel yourself forward along your career path of choice.

In this chapter you'll learn:

- The benefits of storytelling in a professional setting
- Why storytelling during a transition is important
- What makes a compelling story
- How to write your core story
- Tactics for compelling storytelling
- How to write your elevator pitch

THE BENEFITS OF STORYTELLING FOR YOUR CAREER

Why have a core story?

Well, facts don't speak for themselves. The cold, hard truth isn't memorable, persuasive or unique.

But stories are.

They are a way to break through the clutter of information we're bombarded with every day and present your facts in a new way - a way that is meaningful and provides context.

A story helps form a connection between who you are and who (or what) you are targeting.

Stories can:

- Help you make a positive impression, quickly
- Boost your perceived authenticity
- Hint at the best parts of your nature, without having to brag
- Demonstrate your people skills (which storytelling is a natural part of)
- Accentuate similarities between yourself and your listener
- Distinguish you from the crowd - it's good marketing!
- Help others get inside your head more than words on a page can
- Inspire others to join you and get on board with your career move

According to Herminia Ibarra and Kent Lineback, contributors to *Harvard Business Review*, stories that resonate:

- "Help listeners feel they have a stake in our success"
- "Help us believe in ourselves"
- "Reassure us that our plans make sense"
- "Give us motivation and help us endure frustration, suffering and hard work"[1]

These factors are perhaps never more important than during a career transition.

STORYTELLING DURING TRANSITIONS

For those leaping into a new career, your core story is critical. Aside from relying on cold, hard facts to drive a story, there's another common mistake. That is: playing it safe.

People worry that if their story projects anything other than complete stability, they won't look attractive in an employer's eyes. Unfortunately, this "safe" appearance only casts them in one light - unremarkable.

Instead, you need to emphasise transformation. But, how to do this in a way that is still reassuring to the listener?

The answer lies in story coherence to convince the reader that the change in career makes sense. To properly explain transformation, it's best not to use external reasons (like being let go), but internal ones of self-discovery and learning - both of which are inspiring to hear about.

TACTICS FOR WRITING COMPELLING STORIES

The best stories contain obstacles that the hero (i.e.

you) must overcome. Your core story is no different. It should make the listener feel something, which will then translate into a memory for them. After all, one of the most important things during a job search is staying in the front of mind.

If you have the opportunity to learn a little about the person asking you questions beforehand, you'll be able to take advantage of the "reminding me of me" tactic. According to Esther Choy, author of *Let the Story do the Work*, when people ask "tell me about yourself" what they really mean is "tell me something about yourself that reminds me of me."[2]

If you don't have the opportunity to learn about them beforehand, then your story should reflect something that is universal.

What your audience is likely to remember the most is the ending of your story. So when you're writing, ask yourself what you hope they will take away, and ensure your ending satisfies that.

You also want it to be positive and upbeat. In the context of a career search, even though there should be an obstacle, the overall feeling should uplift and inspire. After all, when you're making choices in your career to enrich your life, how you project yourself should be in line with that.

HOW TO WRITE YOUR CORE STORY

How do you tie your achievements, skills, interests, values and motivations together? I suggest you wrap this up into one core story for you to remember and articulate as your personal brand. Your core story is your benchmark against which you can remember and also evaluate.

Consider: which one core achievement stands out the most to you. Which one, if you replicated it time and time again, would make you happiest? Which one has the most elements that define you?

This will become your core story - your benchmark against which choices can be made confidently and a way for you to authentically convey who you are and what you're about.

If you're struggling to decide between two or more achievements, be hard on yourself. Work out the one and only one.

ACTION STEPS

Start by answering these questions:

1. What is your core achievement? Refer back to your answers in Chapter 4.

_____

_____

_____

_____

_____

2. What triggered you to start on your own journey?

_____

_____

_____

_____

_____

3. What stories along the way helped to reinforce that your journey was on the right path for you?

_____

_____

_____

_____

_____

4. What do you believe in?

_____
_____
_____
_____
_____
_____

5. What have you dedicated your life to?

_____
_____
_____
_____
_____
_____

6. What are you committed to?

_____
_____
_____
_____
_____
_____

7. Why do you get out of bed in the morning, and why should anyone care?

_____
_____
_____
_____
_____
_____

8. What is the visceral, core reason you do what you do?

_____
_____
_____
_____
_____
_____

9. From these answers, write your core story. Then review it. You might need to rewrite it to also encompass your core skills, interests, values and motivations, from your answers in Chapters 4-6.

_____
_____
_____
_____
_____

10. Say it out loud - it should be less than two minutes. When you're comfortable with it, then you're there.

_____

_____

_____

_____

_____

_____

COMPELLING STORYTELLING TACTICS

Once you have written your core story, the battle's only half won, because telling the story is just as important. According to Stephen Denning, author of *The Leader's Guide to Storytelling*, there are four key elements to storytelling:

1. **Style:** You need to be focused, clear and giving all your attention to the one person you are speaking to.

2. **Truth:** you're not arguing a point in a debate. You are presenting the truth as simply and succinctly as you can.

3. **Preparation:** you need to be rehearsed enough to present your story's key elements in the right order, but not so much so that it loses all meaning and inflection when you deliver it.

4. **Delivery:** 93% of meaning is derived from non-verbal communication, a 1973 study found. So remember that the impression you leave will come down considerably to how you tell the story.[3]

Brian Boyd, author of *On the Origin of Stories: Evolution, Cognition, and Fiction*, writes a story is "a thing that does" rather than "a thing that is."[4]

A core story is more dynamic than an elevator pitch - but you'll need both!

YOUR ELEVATOR PITCH

Even if you're between jobs, it doesn't mean you shouldn't have an elevator pitch. After all, once you've established your new career direction, you can tailor your elevator pitch to reflect where you are now and where you'd like to go.

An elevator statement or pitch is a concise, well-rehearsed summary of your value proposition. Metaphorically, we all know an elevator statement or pitch should be delivered in 30 - 90 seconds - the time it takes an elevator to ride from the ground floor to the top floor.

If you are not comfortable with the elevator analogy, another way to think about it is a 'BBQ Statement', or a 'Pub Pitch'. So, whether you're having a chat while cooking a steak at a BBQ or it's over a beer at the pub, this is about helping the recipient of your pitch 'get you' in the first few seconds of their time with you.

The traditional elevator pitch is a conversation killer. As soon as you hand over your job title, people have

judged you, filled in the blanks according to their existing beliefs and moved on. It's essentially all over.

That's why Choy advocates giving your audience a gift: "the opportunity to use their imaginations." That gift is storytelling.[5]

Specifically, Choy suggests using one storytelling tactic in particular - a hook.

You can create a hook by using terminology that isn't characteristic for your industry. Choy gives these excellent examples for those established in a career:

- I protect audiences from boring speakers (speechwriter)
- I'm a real estate treasure hunter (real estate hedge fund manager)[6]

Here are a few ideas for graduates in an area of specialisation, but who haven't started their career as yet:

- I help property developers optimise their investment portfolio (graduate developer)
- I keep the taxman out of your hip pocket (graduate accountant)
- I create smooth roads (graduate surveyor)

The trick is in not being too obtuse and off-putting. When people have no experience with the industry or type of work you've been doing or are about to do, they are easily confused. You want to make them sizzlingly curious, so to do that, they need to understand what you've said - but the trick lies in still making it interesting enough that people ask you to clarify further.

Ideally, you don't want to deliver your elevator pitch all in one, but consider using it as the framework for a dialogue.

For instance, you would deliver your introductory line like "I protect audiences from boring speakers" to pique their interest. Then they'll ask you to clarify, and you can continue with your pitch.

If you're having trouble finding the right balance for this hook, I suggest you instead use a formula

that I originally saw in Allan Dib's book, *'The 1 Page Marketing Plan'*[7]. I call it the PSP framework, which looks like this:

You know (Problem)? **P**
Well, what I do is (Solution). **S**
In fact (Proof). **P**

You know **P** ?

Well, what I do is **S** .

In fact **P** .

You always introduce the problem with
"You know how ..."

You always introduce the solution with
"Well what I do is ..."

You always provide proof with
"In fact, ..."

Here are three examples to guide you in developing your own elevator statement:

For a tax accountant:

You know how people pay too much income tax.

Well, what I do is legally reduce tax for all my personal and corporate clients.

In fact, I just reduced the income tax for a company that paid a $2 million tax bill the prior year to $1 million and for one personal client I was even able to get him a refund.

For a mortgage broker:

You know how most people finance their home and continue to pay that mortgage year-in, year-out without questioning that arrangement.

Well, what I do is help people know what the latest mortgage offerings are in the market and how they could roll over from their existing provider to a better provider.

In fact, just last week, a client of mine was able to reduce his annual mortgage repayments by over $7,000 by switching to the provider I recommended.

For a payroll manager:

You know how one of the most annoying and disengaging things any employer can do is incorrectly process employee's pay. It peeves the employee and ties up the employer's payroll department's resources.

Well, what I do is to make sure every payroll run complies with all awards and contracts, consistently providing error-free processing.

In fact, in the last year, I've been able to reduce the number of calls our Payroll Department receives from 100 complaints per payroll run to zero.

The PSP (Problem, Solution, Proof) Elevator Statement framework works better than most other frameworks I've encountered.

It's simple.
It's easy to understand.
It does not take a lot of effort to learn.

Now, it's over to you.

ACTION STEPS

Develop your own Elevator Statement for your potential
new role

1. "You know (Problem)? P

_____
_____
_____
_____
_____
_____

2. Well, what I do is (Solution). S

_____
_____
_____
_____
_____
_____

3. In fact (Proof)." P

_____
_____
_____
_____
_____
_____

4. Create a hook to try out as well

_____

_____

_____

_____

_____

_____

Start testing one or two versions of your elevator pitch to see how your audience responds. Keep track of your responses. Ideally, you'll find that as you tweak it over time and become more natural in delivery, your engagement will improve.

KEY LESSONS

Before you proceed to the next chapter, I encourage you to revisit these lessons from the chapter you just read.

Being able to convey who you are in a succinct and engaging manner has many benefits in a professional setting. Using elements of storytelling in your core story and elevator pitch can help you realise these benefits including:

- Making fast and positive first impressions
- Conveying your authenticity to develop connections
- Distinguish you from the crowd
- Show you are memorable
- And perhaps most importantly, inspire others to get on board with your career move

Your core story should be centred around one core achievement, but tie in with your skills, interests, values and motivations too - to give a more complete picture of your professional identity.

It should see you overcome an obstacle, to have an uplifting ending that creates a feeling in the listener that will come back to them whenever you come to mind.

An elevator pitch is a way for you to answer the question, "so what do you do" even more succinctly than a core story.

Following this framework:

You know (Problem)? **P**
Well, what I do is (Solution). **S**
In fact (Proof). **P**

will help you convey in 90 seconds or less where you are now and even where you're hoping to go.

CONVEY WHO YOU ARE

Chapter 12 brings us to the conclusion of our time together, for now, as you embark on your path of re-launching or re-dedication.

CHAPTER 12

CONCLUSION

Career stagnation can feel much like bobbing in the ocean, cast adrift in a rudderless boat. The more time that passes, the more depleted you feel, directionless and with no land in sight.

If you only had the help of sails and a rudder, you could soon navigate your way back to shore.

That's what this book is intended to be. Each action step is intended to act as a rudder to guide you forward, discover what energises you and show you that your ideal career is within sight.

So having reached the final chapter of this book, I want to congratulate you.

It's time to cry, "Land, ho!"

You're either about to start seeking opportunities for your newly-discovered ideal job or re-dedicate yourself with vigour to your current career path.

But for now, I'd like you to pause a few moments and imagine what your future with this chosen career is going to look like.

Specifically, what would it mean to you if:

- You were able to get out of bed each morning *without* dreading going to work
- You had a job you felt proud of and found satisfaction in doing
- Your time spent at work didn't feel wasted, but as though it was an integral component of who you are
- Your career helped to enrich your life
- You had the opportunity to master an area of interest to you
- You could dedicate yourself to lifelong learning
- You had a job that allows for relatedness, competency and autonomy
- You were employable long-term
- You finally had a job you want to do, not just have to

While there isn't such a thing as a perfect job, I can say with certainty that there are multiple ideal career pathways for everyone.

You've been making choices throughout this book to identify the aspects you find enriching and those that add value to your life while minimising those that deplete your energy. Let's refresh your memory about them for a moment.

MAXIMISE WHAT ENRICHES YOU

Philosopher and civil rights leader Howard W. Thurman said, "ask what makes you come alive and go do it."

The building blocks that form you as a person, are your clues to finding a fulfilling career. In particular, those building blocks should be what makes you come alive, satisfies you, and brings a sense of pride, joy and inspiration.

Choosing a career direction based on your most enriching skills, achievements, interests, values, motivations and who you fit with gives you the opportunity to develop passion in a job, rather than expecting the world to offer passion up to you.

If you are innately purpose-driven, then looking to *why* you do what you do can elevate your enriched career even further.

As for *your* journey of career discovery, you may find yourself at a fork in the road: whether to remain on your current path or turn in a new direction.

HAVE YOU DECIDED TO RE-DEDICATE OR RE-LAUNCH?

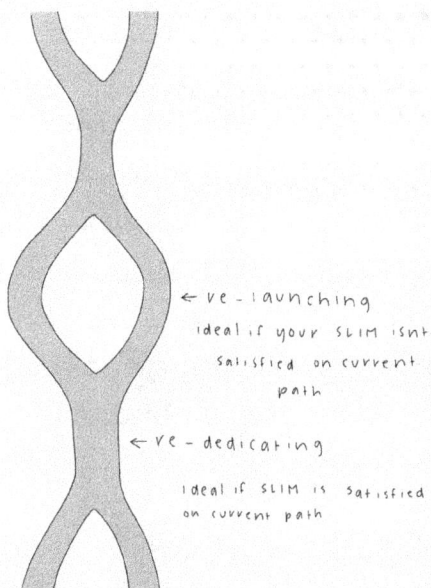

← re-launching
ideal if your SLIM isnt satisfied on current path

← re-dedicating
ideal if SLIM is satisfied on current path

You could choose to rededicate if you've realised that (with some minor adjustments) your current career path can satisfy the criteria for an enriched career for you, namely, the intersection of **S**trengths + **L**ove + **I**mportance + **M**oney (SLIM). This decision makes your road ahead very clear, so now you'll need to invest some time to plan how you will make those adjustments happen.

On the other hand, relaunching your career is ideal if you're seeking change - whether that be because your current or prior career is unsatisfying, or if you've decided to take a new path that holds the

potential to bring a sense of enrichment to your life like never before.

Each of these paths requires a commitment to lifelong learning in order to maintain relevance in a world that demands long-term employability over long-term employment. As well as mastering an area of interest to you, commitment to lifelong learning allows you to build value by intersecting your primary area of expertise with knowledge and skills from other fields too. It gives you the opportunity to stay up to date or even ahead of the curve.

It's an exciting commitment in terms of your own development and confidence in your abilities, and it also distinguishes you as a valuable employee who potential employers would be lucky to have.

There are, of course, additional ways to become an employee of value and therefore, employable long-term.

They include:

- Portability
- Determination
- Self-awareness
- Possessing a craftsman mindset

Whichever approach you take toward your career now, whether that's rededication or relaunching, I want you to remember that it isn't for life - so you don't need to feel daunted about making that one and only, perfect decision. You will likely need to move between emergent and deliberate strategies at different times in order to enjoy both long-term fulfilment and employability.

So, be excited about the possibilities!

ARE YOU CLEAR ON YOUR SLIMPACT™?

SLIMPACT

In Chapter 8 I showed you how to combine everything you've learned about yourself and apply my proven framework for identifying an enriching career through the lens of the SLIMPACT™ model.

Working on your SLIMPACT™ is the most critical lesson contained within this book for finding a career that contributes to an overall enriched and fulfilled life, rather than a depleted one.

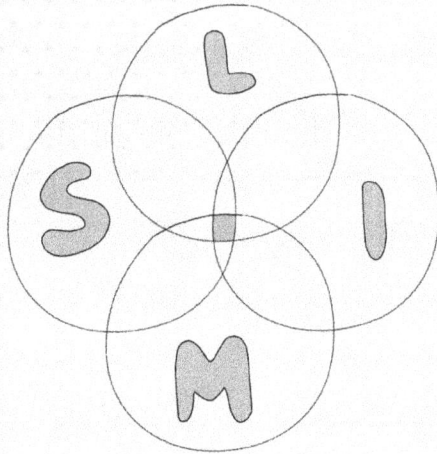

Remember, your enriched career is found at the intersection of:

- **Strengths:** What you are naturally good at, or have worked hard to develop skills in
- **Love:** What you do that interests and excites you
- **Importance:** What you stand for and the working culture you best fit with
- **Money:** What is financially viable for you to do as a career

And if you are purpose-driven, your super- enriched career also intersects with:

- **Purpose:** *Why* you do what you do and the desire to create an impact bigger than yourself

If working on your SLIMPACT™ has led you to a new path to pursue, I'm so excited for you!

You're taking action to lead a life enriched by all that you do.

You'll enjoy the many benefits of finding your ideal career path, like:

- Higher engagement with your job
- Greater job satisfaction
- Opportunities for further growth and development

One last piece of advice I would give in relation to your own SLIMPACT™ is not to compromise! Go after what you want with determination, because you deserve a career that fills all your buckets.

Speaking of buckets, I urge you to take the time to test the waters of your potential career paths before diving in, if you haven't done so yet. This will help you ensure your assumptions of the job are realistic, that you are as interested in the industry as you think you are, and identify where or how you can be of most value, so you really make an impression when you commit.

YOUR NEXT STEPS

So, where to from here?

(**1**) If you're already making inroads into your new career and would like help maximising your success during the onboarding period, see my new book: ***So You Got the Job: WTF is Next?***

(**2**) How did you go?

Please share how your transition goes. I'd love to hear how this book helped you find your enriched career and navigate the road ahead.

Email me at **gregw@wtfisnext.wtf**

(**3**) Looking for additional resources?

Visit **wtfisnext.wtf**

I wish you well in your newfound and enriching career discovery!

FOOTNOTES

Introduction

1   https://www.seek.com.au/career-advice/how-long-does-it-really-take-to-find-a-new-job

2   https://www.randstadusa.com/jobs/career-resources/career-advice/the-art-of-the-job-hunt/631/

3   https://www.executiveconnexions.com/job-search/long-executive-job-search-take/

4   https://www.forbes.com/sites/jeannemeister/2012/08/14/the-future-of-work-job-hopping-is-the-new-normal-for-millennials/#7bdc833513b8

5   https://www.theglobeandmail.com/report-on-business/careers/management/is-workplace-loyalty-dead-in-the-age-of-the-millennial/article36675517/

6   https://www.forbes.com/sites/jacobmorgan/2014/03/20/5-reasons-why-long-term-employment-is-dead-and-never-coming-back/#4351c23c34e4

7   https://www.nytimes.com/2011/04/24/jobs/24search.html

8   https://www.nytimes.com/2011/04/24/jobs/24search.html

9   "The World is Flat" by T. L. Friedman. Published by Farrar, Straus and Giroux, 2005.

10   https://www.learningsolutionsmag.com/articles/2468/marc-my-words-the-coming-knowledge-tsunami

11   https://www.forbes.com/sites/lizryan/2014/12/27/five-ways-full-time-employment-can-hurt-you/#6c104b4443ce

12   http://www.forbes.com/sites/lizryan/2014/07/17/how-to-tell-dragon-slaying-stories-on-a-job-interview/

13   https://www.forbes.com/sites/lizryan/2014/12/27/five-ways-full-time-employment-can-hurt-you/#6c104b4443ce

14   https://www.forbes.com/sites/lizryan/2014/12/27/five-ways-full-time-employment-can-hurt-you/#6c104b4443ce

15   https://medium.com/thrive-global/ikigai-the-japanese-secret-to-a-long-and-happy-life-might-just-help-you-live-a-more-fulfilling-9871d01992b7

16   https://www.psychologytoday.com/au/blog/design-your-path/201206/the-immense-pressure-career-choice

Chapter 1

1   https://www.psychologytoday.com/au/articles/201209/the-siren-call-starting-over

2   https://www.psychologytoday.com/au/articles/201209/the-siren-call-starting-over

3   https://www.psychologytoday.com/au/articles/201209/the-siren-call-starting-over

4   https://www.psychologytoday.com/au/blog/two-minute-shrink/201003/are-you-still-suffering-memories-unpleasant-experience

5   https://www.helpguide.org/articles/stress/job-loss-and-unemployment-stress.htm/

6   https://hbr.org/2016/04/navigating-the-emotional-side-of-a-career-transition

7   https://hbr.org/ideacast/2018/11/how-your-identity-changes-when-you-change-jobs

8   https://www.delltechnologies.com/content/dam/delltechnologies/assets/perspectives/2030/pdf/SR1940_IFTFforDellTechnologies_Human-Machine_070517_readerhigh-res.pdf

9   "On Death and Dying" by E. Kubler-Ross. Published by Taylor & Francis, Ltd, 2008.

Chapter 2

1   "On Death and Dying" by E. Kubler-Ross. Published by Taylor & Francis, Ltd, 2008.

2   "The Reality Slap" by R. Harris. Published by Exisle Publishing, 2011.

3   https://www.psychologytoday.com/us/blog/cutting-

edge-leadership/201405/why-grads-experience-post-graduation-letdown

4   https://www.washingtonpost.com/national/health-science/theres-such-a-thing-as-post-graduation-depression-i-know-i-had-it/2017/08/04/4d163c6a-618d-11e7-a4f7-af34fc1d9d39_story.html?noredirect=on&utm_term=.b37607721c4f

5   https://www.washingtonpost.com/national/health-science/theres-such-a-thing-as-post-graduation-depression-i-know-i-had-it/2017/08/04/4d163c6a-618d-11e7-a4f7-af34fc1d9d39_story.html?noredirect=on&utm_term=.b37607721c4f

6   http://content.time.com/time/health/article/0,8599,1896986,00.html

7   "The Happiness Trap" by R. Harris. Published by Exisle Publishing, 2013.

Chapter 3

1   "Why People Fail" by S. Reynolds. Published by John Wiley & Sons, 2011.

2   "The Happiness Trap" by R. Harris. Published by Exisle Publishing, 2013.

3   "The Happiness Trap" by R. Harris. Published by Exisle Publishing, 2013.

4   https://hbr.org/2011/04/building-resilience

5   https://hbr.org/2011/04/building-resilience

6   "The Reality Slap" by R. Harris. Published by Exisle Publishing, 2011.

7   https://www.psychologytoday.com/au/blog/fulfillment-any-age/201204/give-your-career-mindset-tune

8   https://www.psychologytoday.com/au/blog/fulfillment-any-age/201204/give-your-career-mindset-tune

9   https://www.psychologytoday.com/au/blog/fulfillment-any-age/201204/give-your-career-mindset-tune

Chapter 4

1 https://hbr.org/2013/04/the-key-to-choosing-the-right

2 "How Will You Measure Your Life" by C. Christensen, J. Allworth & K. Dillon. Published by HarperCollins, 2012.

3 "Self-Determination Theory: Basic Psychological Needs in Motivation, Development, and Wellness" by R. Ryan and E. Deci. Published by The Guilford Press, 2018.

4 "So Good They Can't Ignore You" by C. Newport. Published by Piatkus, 2016.

5 "The Art of Achievement" by T. Morris. Published by Andrew McMeel Publishing, LLC, 2013.

6 "The Art of Achievement" by T. Morris. Published by Andrew McMeel Publishing, LLC, 2013.

7 "The Art of Achievement" by T. Morris. Published by Andrew McMeel Publishing, LLC, 2013.

8 http://unsettle.org/skills/

9 http://unsettle.org/skills/

10 https://www.forbes.com/sites/anneglusker/2018/06/08/why-people-skills-are-so-important-and-how-you-can-polish-yours-to-a-shine/#62f237c62458

11 https://www.psychologytoday.com/au/blog/communication-success/201410/how-increase-your-emotional-intelligence-6-essentials

12 https://www.psychologytoday.com/au/blog/communication-success/201410/how-increase-your-emotional-intelligence-6-essentials

13 https://www.naturalhr.com/2017/10/10/emotional-intelligence-important/

14 https://www.viacharacter.org/www/

15 https://www.zora.uzh.ch/id/eprint/63535/1/174_m_2012_HarzerRuch.pdf

16 "Why People Fail" by S. Reynolds. Published by Penguin, 2012.

17 "So Good They Can't Ignore You" by C. Newport. Published by Piatkus, 2016.

Chapter 5

1. https://www.forbes.com/sites/ forbeswomanfiles/2014/07/02/3-practical-ways- to-find-your-lifes-passion-and-a-career-you- love/#78b8de4f1413

2. https://hbr.org/2018/09/having-a-growth-mindset- makes-it-easier-to-develop-new-interests

Chapter 6

1. https://www.stevepavlina.com/blog/2004/11/list-of- values/

2. "Focus" by H. Grant Halvorson and E. Tory Higgins. Published by Hudson Street Press, 2013.

3. https://hbr.org/2013/03/do-you-play-to-win-or-to-not- lose

4. https://hbr.org/2013/03/do-you-play-to-win-or-to-not- lose

5. https://hbr.org/2013/04/the-key-to-choosing-the-right

6. "Self-Determination Theory: Basic Psychological Needs in Motivation, Development, and Wellness" by R. Ryan and E. Deci. Published by The Guilford Press, 2018.

7. "Succeed: How We Can Reach Our Goals" by H. Grant Halvorson and C. Dweck. Published by Plume 2010.

8. "It's Not the How or the What But the Who" by C. Fernandez-Araoz. Published by Harvard Business Review Press, 2014.

9. https://www.naturalhr.com/2017/10/10/emotional- intelligence-important/

10. "Thinking Fast and Slow" by D. Kahneman. Published by Penguin, 2011.

11. "It's Not the How or the What But the Who" by C. Fernandez-Araoz. Published by Harvard Business Review Press, 2014.

12. "Thinking Fast and Slow" by D. Kahneman. Published by Penguin, 2011.

13 "It's Not the How or the What But the Who" by C. Fernandez-Araoz. Published by Harvard Business Review Press, 2014.

14 "Thinking Fast and Slow" by D. Kahneman. Published by Penguin, 2011.

15 https://hbr.org/2017/11/how-to-tell-if-a-companys-culture-is-right-for-you

16 http://ideonomy.mit.edu/essays/traits.html

Chapter 7

1 "Designing Your Life" by B. Burnett & D. Evans. Published by Vintage Digital, 2016.

2 https://www.ted.com/talks/scott_dinsmore_how_to_find_work_you_love/transcript?language=en

3 "Barking Up the Wrong Tree" by E. Barker. Published by HarperOne, 2017.

4 "Designing Your Life" by B. Burnett & D. Evans. Published by Vintage Digital, 2016.

5 https://hbr.org/2003/01/one-more-time-how-do-you-motivate-employees

6 "How Will You Measure Your Life" by C. Christensen, J. Allworth & K. Dillon. Published by HarperCollins, 2012.

7 https://www.theseus.fi/bitstream/handle/10024/113325/Thesis%20-%20Essi%20Vuokko%20-%20Print.pdf?sequence=1

Chapter 8

1 "Self-Determination Theory: Basic Psychological Needs in Motivation, Development, and Wellness" by R. Ryan and E. Deci. Published by The Guilford Press, 2018.

2 "Self-Determination Theory: Basic Psychological Needs in Motivation, Development, and Wellness" by R. Ryan and E. Deci. Published by The Guilford Press, 2018.

3 "Designing Your Life" by B. Burnett & D. Evans. Published by Vintage Digital, 2016.

4   "Designing Your Life" by B. Burnett & D. Evans. Published by Vintage Digital, 2016.

5   "Start With Why" by S. Sinek. Published by Penguin, 2011.

6   "Making Hope Happen" by S. J. Lopez. Published by Atria Books, 2013.

7   "Mastery" by R Greene. Published by Profile Books, 2012.

Chapter 9

1   "It's Not the How or the What But the Who" by C. Fernandez-Araoz. Published by Harvard Business Review Press, 2014.

2   https://hbr.org/2013/07/craft-a-sustainable-career

3   "It's Not the How or the What But the Who" by C. Fernandez-Araoz. Published by Harvard Business Review Press, 2014.

4   https://www.fya.org.au/wp-content/uploads/2016/11/The-New-Work-Mindset.pdf

5   https://cica.org.au/fya-releases-the-new-work-mindset-report/

6   https://www.fya.org.au/wp-content/uploads/2016/11/The-New-Work-Mindset.pdf

7   "It's Not the How or the What But the Who" by C. Fernandez-Araoz. Published by Harvard Business Review Press, 2014.

8   https://hbr.org/2013/07/craft-a-sustainable-career

9   "So Good They Can't Ignore You" by C. Newport. Published by Piatkus, 2016.

10   "So Good They Can't Ignore You" by C. Newport. Published by Piatkus, 2016.

11   https://www.mckinsey.com/industries/social-sector/our-insights/education-to-employment-designing-a-system-that-works

12   "Mastery" by R Greene. Published by Profile Books, 2012.

13   https://first20hours.com/

14   https://first20hours.com/

15   "How Will You Measure Your Life" by C. Christensen, J. Allworth & K. Dillon. Published by HarperCollins, 2012.

16   "How Will You Measure Your Life" by C. Christensen, J. Allworth & K. Dillon. Published by HarperCollins, 2012.

Chapter 10

1   "How Will You Measure Your Life" by C. Christensen, J. Allworth & K. Dillon. Published by HarperCollins, 2012.

2   "How Will You Measure Your Life" by C. Christensen, J. Allworth & K. Dillon. Published by HarperCollins, 2012.

3   "Designing Your Life" by B. Burnett & D. Evans. Published by Vintage Digital, 2016.

4   "Designing Your Life" by B. Burnett & D. Evans. Published by Vintage Digital, 2016.

5   "The New Rules of Work: The Modern Playbook for Navigating Your Career" by A. Cavoulacos and K. Minshew. Published by Crown Business, 2017.

6   "Mastery" by R Greene. Published by Profile Books, 2012.

7   https://hbr.org/2011/02/demystifying-mentoring

8   https://hbr.org/2011/02/demystifying-mentoring

9   https://www.psychologytoday.com/us/blog/the-blame-game/201607/decision-making-made-ridiculously-simple

Chapter 11

1   https://hbr.org/2005/01/whats-your-story

2   "Let the Story Do the Work" by E. Choy. Published by AMACOM, 2017.

3   "The Leader's Guide to Storytelling" by S. Denning. Published by Jossey-Bass, 2011.

4   "On the Origin of Stories: Evolution, Cognition, and Fiction" by B. Boyd. Published by Belknap Press, 2010.

5 "Let the Story Do the Work" by E. Choy. Published by AMACOM, 2017.

6 "Let the Story Do the Work" by E. Choy. Published by AMACOM, 2017.

7 https://successwise.com/book/

INDEX

R

S

T

V

www.ingramcontent.com/pod-product-compliance
Lightning Source LLC
Chambersburg PA
CBHW071334210326
41597CB00015B/1446